WELCOME

The transatlantic slave trade is one of the most shameful chapters in human history. Between 1500 and 1900 it's estimated that around 12 million African men, women, and children were stolen from their homes by Europeans, before being forcefully transported thousands of miles across the Atlantic. Those who survived the horrific 'Middle Passage' would then be sold, often separated from their families, and put to work as enslaved labor on plantations throughout the New World. While this inhumane trade was eventually abolished in the 19th century, the scars still remain and the lasting impact is still being felt by communities around the world.

In this bookazine, we seek to tell the story of the transatlantic slave trade – from its origins to its abolition. We discover the impact on Africa, the horrors of the Middle Passage, and what life was like for millions of enslaved people. We also look to explore the legacies of slavery and how the effects are still being felt in the modern world.

CONTENTS

◆

STORY OF THE SLAVE TRADE

THE HUMAN EXPERIENCE

HISTORY OF THE
AVE TRADE

RIGINS OF THE SLAVE TRADE AND ITS IMPACTS OUGHOUT HISTORY AND THE PRESENT DAY

EDOARDO ALBERT

HARETH AL BUSTANI

JOSEPHINE HALL

FOX CHAPEL
PUBLISHING

©2023 by Future Publishing Limited

Articles in this issue are translated or reproduced from *History of the Slave Trade* and are the copyright of or licensed to Future Publishing Limited, a Future plc group company, UK 2022.

Used under license. All rights reserved. This version published by Fox Chapel Publishing Company, Inc., 903 Square Street, Mount Joy, PA 17552.

For more information about the Future plc group, go to http://www.futureplc.com.

ISBN 978-1-4971-0398-6

Library of Congress Cataloging-in-Publication Data

To learn more about the other great books from Fox Chapel Publishing, or to find a retailer near you, call toll-free 800-457-9112 or visit us at www.FoxChapelPublishing.com.

We are always looking for talented authors. To submit an idea, please send a brief inquiry to acquisitions@foxchapelpublishing.com.

Printed in China
First printing

84

96

62

44

18

BLM

6

118

FIGHT FOR FREEDOM

LEGACY & IMPACT

Images: Getty Images (p20, p30, p92, p98), Alamy (p54, p64, p86, p116, p120)

THE TRANSATLANTIC SLAVE TRADE TIMELINE

European economic development and the exploitation of resources in the Americas fuelled the emergence of the African slave trade

THE PORTUGUESE INITIATE TRANSATLANTIC SLAVE TRADE
1526
Trade route from Africa to Brazil

The first known English slave trader, Sir John Hawkins, also established the transatlantic triangular trade route

SIR JOHN HAWKINS ESTABLISHES ENGLISH SLAVE TRADE
1562-69
Trade routes from England to Africa and the New World

Conducting three voyages from England to Sierra Leone on the coast of West Africa and then to the island of Hispaniola, Sir John Hawkins is the first Englishman considered to be actively involved in the transatlantic slave trade. His voyages establish the triangular trade route, standard for more than two centuries. Ships depart ports in England and other European countries laden with goods to be traded for slaves on the African coast. The slaves are then transported across the Atlantic Ocean via the notorious Middle Passage and sold as laborers to plantation owners in the New World. Completing the triangle, ships transport commodities such as cotton, sugar, rum, tobacco, and coffee back to Europe.

Portuguese slave traders pay respects to an African king as they ply their trade

Prominent Boston landmark Faneuil Hall was built by slaver Peter Faneuil, who conducted slave auctions nearby

MASSACHUSETTS LEGALIZES SLAVERY

December 10, 1641
Boston, Massachusetts

A slave owner himself, Governor John Winthrop is a principal author of the Massachusetts Bodies of Liberty, the first collection of laws that legalize the institution of slavery in North America. Samuel Maverick, an owner of two slaves, had brought them to the English colony in 1624, while the first slaves imported directly to Massachusetts from Africa made their arrival in 1634. In 1638, the slave ship Desire had brought enslaved Africans from Barbados in the Caribbean, and these were exchanged for members of the Pequot tribe captured in New England and placed in bondage. Between 1755 and 1764, the number of slaves in Massachusetts rises to 2.2 percent of the total population.

Massachusetts governor John Winthrop was a slaveholder and contributor to laws legalizing slavery in the colony

SLAVES INTRODUCED AT JAMESTOWN

August 20, 1619
Jamestown, Virginia

Sailing from the Caribbean, an English privateer, the White Lion, reaches Point Comfort, now Hampton Roads, not far from Jamestown, Virginia, the first permanent English-speaking colony in North America. They trade 20 African slaves for food and other provisions. These are the first slaves imported to Britain's North American colonies. During a span of four centuries, an estimated 12 to 13 million enslaved Africans are brought to North and South America by European traders to toil as field workers, house servants, and laborers.

Arriving at Jamestown, Virginia, aboard the White Lion in 1619, African slaves cower near the shore

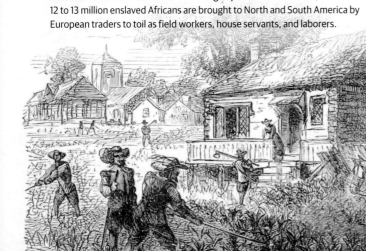

In colonial Virginia, tobacco became a lucrative cash crop. Slave labor was instrumental in its production

Of Human Bondage

Slavery, or involuntary servitude, has been an element of civilization for thousands of years

From earliest recorded history, the concept of slavery or involuntary servitude has existed, transcending cultural or ethical conditions and enabling those who have exploited human suffering to build immense wealth and exert control over subservient peoples.

With the emergence of social classes, slavery developed in Sumeria and Mesopotamia, even being referenced in the Code of Hammurabi as an institution with its purpose and place in society. The development of slavery in civilization stemmed from the need for labor, simply the performance of functions that contributed to the augmentation of wealth or the increase of status. Slaves were either captured during raids and transported to markets to be sold as commodities, taken prisoner during battles among rival kingdoms or empires and cast into bondage as the spoils of war, sold or surrendered by next of kin to serve a monarch or person of high social status, or punished for some egregious crime.

From 3,500 BCE forward, records of slave enterprises in Sumeria have survived. Biblical references to slavery abound, particularly that of the Hebrew people delivered by God from bondage in Egypt. Slavery cast its shadow across the glory of the Roman Empire and the magnificence of classical Greece. Examples of slavery and involuntary servitude in ancient China and other Asian cultures attest that the institution has not been confined only to Western civilization, and that the transatlantic slave trade was an extension of a practice that predated its horrors for centuries. Numerous African kingdoms, in fact, held slavery in high regard, even revered the concept of enslaving the vanquished of neighboring empires following military victories. Slavery, therefore, is as old as civilization itself, a symptom of the human condition – and one of its basest elements.

Trudging along in chains, Roman slaves are led toward an ancient and uncertain future

ROYAL AFRICAN COMPANY CHARTERED

September 24, 1672
London, England

King Charles II grants a charter to the Royal African Company, effectively a monopoly of the English slave trade on the west coast of Africa from the Cape of Good Hope to the western reaches of the Sahara Desert. The Royal African Company is led by the Duke of York, the future King James II and brother of King Charles II. Financed by numerous aristocratic investors, the enterprise will transport more African slaves to the Americas than any other in the history of the transatlantic trade.

King Charles II granted his brother, future King James II, leadership of the Royal African Company

GRANVILLE SHARP INITIATES LEGAL CHALLENGE TO BRITISH SLAVE TRADE
1765
London, England

TOUSSAINT L'OUVERTURE LEADS SLAVE UPRISING IN SAINT DOMINGUE
1791
French Caribbean colony of Saint Domingue

INVENTION OF THE COTTON GIN
1794
Savannah, Georgia

FIRST MAROON WAR

1728-40
Jamaica

While the Caribbean island of Jamaica is under Spanish rule, slaves sometimes escape, reaching the mountains and isolated areas, blending with indigenous peoples, and maintaining a degree of freedom. However, after Britain wrests control of Jamaica from Spain in 1655, revolts erupt and the number of so-called 'maroons' increases. British attempts to quell the unrest and control the entire island escalate into the First Maroon War. Although Britain commits substantial numbers of troops to the pacification effort, a stalemate results in an agreement allowing the maroons to live in certain areas without British interference. In exchange, the maroons are to assist in returning escaped slaves and protecting Jamaica from outside threats.

This armed Jamaican Maroon is typical of those who opposed British pacification efforts

Jamaican Maroons fire on a detachment of British soldiers marching through the jungle

MAROON WAR IN JAMAICA.—P. 175.

STONO REBELLION ERUPTS

September 9, 1739
South Carolina

Jemmy, a literate slave also known as Cato, leads a group of 20 slaves in rebellion along the coast of the South Carolina Lowcountry. From the owner's plantation on the Stono River, Jemmy and his cohorts grow to more than 80 in number, killing up to 25 colonists as they march toward Florida, where the Spanish have promised freedom to slaves who escape the British. However, the South Carolina militia meets the escapees near the Edisto River and suppresses the uprising, killing 35-50 slaves.

The Broadway show *Drumfolk* was inspired by the events of the Stono Rebellion

SLAVE TRADE ACT

March 25, 1807
London, England

Largely due to the efforts of William Wilberforce and his associates, who had taken up the cause of abolishing slavery in Great Britain 20 years earlier, Parliament passes the Slave Trade Act of 1807. Although the act prohibits the slave trade in the British Empire, it does not abolish the practice of slavery; however, Britain urges other nations to consider abolishing its sanction of the slave trade as well. At the time the act is passed, the slave trade remains one of the most profitable business ventures in the Empire, although the institution is not formally ended in Britain until the Slavery Abolition Act of 1833.

In this engraving slave insurrectionist Nat Turner is captured on October 30, 1831

This poignant medallion became the symbol of the British Anti-Slavery Society

William Wilberforce championed the effort to abolish slavery in Great Britain

NAT TURNER'S REBELLION

August 21-23, 1831
Southampton County, Virginia

Slave and preacher Nat Turner leads perhaps the most famous slave uprising in American history. Armed with axes and clubs, Turner and about 70 other slaves began their short-lived rebellion with a murderous rampage, killing more than 50 White people. Although the rebellion is put down at Belmont Plantation within days, Turner remains at large for two months. He is captured and executed amid a wave of retaliation in which approximately 160 Black people are executed by the state of Virginia or murdered.

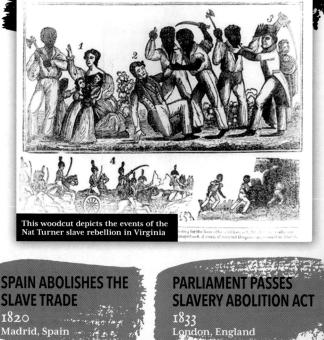

HORRID MASSACRE IN VIRGINIA

This woodcut depicts the events of the Nat Turner slave rebellion in Virginia

THE UNITED STATES BANS AFRICAN SLAVE TRADE
1808
Washington, D.C.

SPAIN ABOLISHES THE SLAVE TRADE
1820
Madrid, Spain

PARLIAMENT PASSES SLAVERY ABOLITION ACT
1833
London, England

Identities of slavery

Slavery and involuntary servitude have existed in numerous forms through the centuries

Slavery is, at its most elementary level, the involuntary coercion or detention of an individual to perform some function for the benefit of others. It has taken many names and has been shrouded in circumstance and suspect justification as well.

While some may have offered the dubious argument that slavery actually has benefitted an enslaved people that otherwise were disadvantaged and unable to competently determine their own future, others have contended that the institution was a necessary tool for the good of society. Therefore, varied genres of slavery have emerged across the millennia.

Slavery encompasses those who were simply seized and sold, those who were captured during wartime and made to serve the victors, and those whose families even considered it a privilege to give their children over to the ruling regime for a lifetime of servitude.

Beyond these concepts, during the colonial era, indentured servitude allowed individuals to seek their own fortune after paying for passage to America with a specified period of work, usually seven years, for the benefit of another. Prisoners, paying their supposed debt to society, have often been employed as laborers, while those who have amassed considerable debt and defaulted have, at times, been sentenced into bondage as a result.

Even today, slavery persists. Although chains may not be visible, millions of people, young and old, are held against their will around the world. Human trafficking for the purposes of cheap labor and illicit sex trade flourishes despite the best efforts of government and law enforcement to eradicate the age-old scourge.

This haunting image titled 'The Slave Market' depicts the despair of those sold into bondage

---

SLAVES SEIZE THE SHIP AMISTAD
1839
Atlantic, near coast of North America

BRAZIL BEGINS ENFORCING LAWS AGAINST SLAVE TRADE
1850
Rio de Janeiro, Brazil

DRED SCOTT DECISION
March 6, 1857
Washington, D.C.

Dred Scott, a slave whose owner transported him from the slave state of Missouri to the free states of Illinois and Wisconsin, sues for his freedom after returning to Missouri, asserting that since he had been transported to free territory he was no longer a slave. After defeat in Missouri state court and US federal court, the case is appealed to the US Supreme Court, which rules 7-2 against Scott. In the landmark decision, Chief Justice Roger B. Taney writes that Blacks "are not included, and were not intended to be included, under the word 'citizens' in the Constitution. . ." and therefore could claim none of the rights of US citizens.

LEFT Slave Dred Scott's quest for freedom reached the United States Supreme Court

ABOVE Chief Justice Roger B. Taney wrote the majority opinion in the landmark Dred Scott decision

The fire engine house at Harpers Ferry has been reconstructed on the original site

JOHN BROWN RAID
October 16-18, 1859
Harpers Ferry, Virginia

Abolitionist John Brown leads 22 men on a raid to seize the federal arsenal at Harpers Ferry, Virginia. Previously involved in other acts of anti-slavery related violence, Brown and several of his men are trapped in the arsenal fire engine house by US Marines under the command of future Confederate General Robert E Lee. One Marine is killed and another wounded, while ten raiders die, seven are captured and five escape. Brown is convicted of treason and executed on December 2, 1859.

Abolitionist firebrand John Brown led the ill-fated raid on the federal arsenal at Harpers Ferry, Virginia

EMANCIPATION PROCLAMATION

January 1, 1863
Washington, D.C.

In the midst of the Civil War and following the tenuous strategic victory on the battlefield of Antietam, President Abraham Lincoln issues the Emancipation Proclamation, ostensibly freeing the slaves held in territories then in rebellion against the United States. The proclamation does not free slaves in the border states of Maryland, Kentucky and Missouri, which remain in the Union, and since the rebellious territories are not fully under Union control, the document serves primarily to add another dimension to the war. Now, not only is the conflict being prosecuted to preserve the Union, but also to end the institution of slavery in the United States.

President Abraham Lincoln issued the Emancipation Proclamation on January 1, 1863

Scars on the back of a slave named Gordon are indicative of the brutality of slavery

Brady   *Washington*

UNITED STATES ABOLISHES SLAVERY

December 6, 1865
Washington, D.C.

The 13th Amendment to the United States Constitution is ratified by 27 of the 36 US states, abolishing slavery and involuntary servitude in the country unless as punishment for a crime. The amendment had been initially proposed on April 8, 1864 and passed the Senate by a vote of 38 to 6. However, it failed in the House of Representatives with a tally of 93 in favor and 65 against, 13 votes short of the two-thirds majority required for passage.

JUNETEENTH COMMEMORATES END OF SLAVERY
June 19, 1865
United States

PORTUGAL ENDS LAST SLAVE ROUTE TO AMERICAS
1870
Lisbon, Portugal

BRAZIL BECOMES THE LAST COUNTRY IN THE AMERICAS TO END SLAVERY
1888
Rio de Janeiro, Brazil

MAJOR CONFEDERATE ARMIES SURRENDER, EFFECTIVELY ENDING AMERICAN CIVIL WAR
1865
Appomattox Court House Virginia; Bennett Place, Durham, North Carolina

Members of the US House of Representatives celebrate the ratification of the 13th Amendment

Representative James Mitchell Ashley of Ohio had proposed a Constitutional amendment to abolish slavery in 1863

The 13th Amendment was just the first of three amendments to be established following the end of the American Civil War

STORY OF THE SLAVE TRADE

*From the origins to abolition, discover the history
of the transatlantic slave trade*

Images: Getty Images (p15, p20, p30), Alamy (p42, p46)

ORIGINS OF THE TRANSATLANTIC SLAVE TRADE

Uncover the little-known genesis of history's darkest trade

● ——— Written by Scott Reeves ——— ●

When Francisco de Rosa looked out on the New World from the deck of the Santa Maria de la Luz, the mariner was satisfied with a job well done. Setting out from Arguim, a tiny island off the coast of what is now Mauritania in West Africa, de Rosa had crossed the Atlantic and made it safely to Puerto Rico with a valuable cargo. Among the goods he carried to sell on the other side of the Atlantic were at least 54 African slaves.

De Rosa's voyage in 1520 was the second known to have been undertaken by a slave ship that sailed direct from Africa to the Americas; he may also have commanded the first slave crossing a year earlier, in which at least 60 slaves were transported. They were among the first voyages in a horrific trade in human beings. By the time that transatlantic slavery came to an end 400 years later, more than 12 million Africans had been forcibly shipped across the ocean. This is the story of the transatlantic slave trade's murky beginnings.

Despite its relative proximity, the African continent beyond the Mediterranean coast was little known to Europeans at the turn of the 15th century. Only when Castilian and Portuguese seafarers began to understand the regular patterns of the Atlantic's currents and winds could they begin to explore to the south in small but maneuverable caravels. Castilians began the conquest of the Canary Islands in 1402;

Portuguese explorers discovered the uninhabited islands of Madeira in 1419, the Azores in 1427 and Cape Verde in 1456.

The new islands had a climate and fertile soil that were perfect for the production of wine and sugar, and were soon settled by pioneering colonists. However, the hard, manual graft required to carve a living on the islands was reserved for others. Although the native Canary Islanders, the Guanches, were an ideal source of labor, it was a limited pool of workers. An alternative source of labor was soon found. In addition to mapping the waters of the east Atlantic, navigators moved down the coast of Africa, pushing beyond the previously known limit of Cape Bojador to reach Cape Blanco in 1441, the Bay of Arguim in 1443, and Cap-Vert in 1444. There they stumbled across a centuries-old trade network in which West African states sold slaves to Arab merchants who transported them across the Sahara to North Africa.

The profits of the trans-Saharan slave trade meant that the West Africa that the Europeans discovered was extremely affluent. By the 14th century the Mali Empire had grown larger than Western Europe. When its leader Mansa Musa visited Cairo on his hajj pilgrimage in 1324, his procession reportedly included 60,000 men, of whom 12,000 were slaves carrying gold bars to pay his way. So vast was his fortune that Musa's party inadvertently caused inflation as prices rocketed in response, devaluing gold for more

The transatlantic slave trade was born when Europeans trafficked enslaved Africans across the Atlantic as labor in the New World

Africa's other slave trade

Slavery was already endemic in African societies when European explorers first came down the west coast. Slaves may have been punished for a crime or debt or were members of a rival tribe who had been captured in war or kidnapped by a raiding party. However, African slaves may have held a different status to those who were unfortunate enough to be chattel slaves on the other side of the Atlantic – they may have had some rights, like owning property and holding public office. When Islam began to spread into Africa in the 7th century, Muslim traders began to range south in search of new markets and partners. Pioneers discovered routes through the Sahara Desert that passed life-preserving oases, often concluding their journeys at Sijilmasa or Kairouan in modern Morocco and Tunisia. Thousands of slaves were taken across the desert each year for use as workers, domestic servants, and concubines in North Africa and the wider Islamic world.

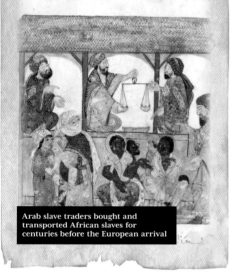

Arab slave traders bought and transported African slaves for centuries before the European arrival

than a decade after his visit. Emperor Askia the Great of the Songhai Empire completed a similarly opulent hajj more than a century later, while the Kingdom of Kongo was an affluent trading state of half a million people with an impressive capital at M'banza-Kongo.

It was tales of such prosperity and gold that drew European explorers to the African coast like moths to a light, eager to trade with the rich rulers. In 1445 the Portuguese established a trading post on a small island in a sheltered bay just off the coast of modern Mauritania. Arguim gave the merchants a base from which they could acquire gold and other commodities, including slaves, who could fetch a decent price

in Europe or the island colonies of the east Atlantic. By 1455 up to 800 slaves a year were being transported from Arguim to Portugal; by the turn of the century some 81,000 slaves had been transported from the African coast on Portuguese ships and as much as ten percent of the population of Lisbon may have been African or of African descent.

The use of Africans as labor in Europe and her colonies provided a steady but small flow of slaves from West African trading ports. However, demand for slaves rocketed after the first explorers returned from the other side of the ocean with tales of vast, unclaimed lands.

When Christopher Columbus discovered Hispaniola – the island containing modern Haiti and the Dominican Republic – in 1492, it was probably home to hundreds of thousands of indigenous inhabitants, the Taíno. However, Spanish colonization was violent. Any natives who opposed the conquerors were mercilessly cut down, while European diseases for which the Taíno had no immunity cut through the population; the first smallpox epidemic in Hispaniola and Puerto Rico may have claimed the lives of around two-thirds of the native population. Within just 30 years, the number of natives plummeted by around 85 percent. By 1514, according to a Spanish census, there were only 26,000 Taíno left under Spanish control. The rich gold mines and agricultural fields that the Spanish had discovered in the New World would be useless if there was nobody to work in them.

It was a situation repeated across the Caribbean – millions of native inhabitants of the islands may have died in the first two or three decades of Spanish expansion. With no local workforce, slaves were shipped from the west coast of Africa to Europe, and from there onto the New World. The first African slaves known to have landed in the Americas reached Hispaniola in 1502, while four African slaves are known to have been shipped from Europe to Cuba in 1513. The Spanish had lost one workforce; their solution was to ship another in from the other side of the ocean.

On August 18. 1518, King Charles I of Spain made the new transatlantic slave trade ruthlessly efficient when he issued a new document that authorized the transportation of slaves direct from Africa to the Americas. The charter allowed Lorenzo de Gorrevod, a trusted advisor and member of the king's council of state, to transport "four thousand Negro slaves both male

SLAVE CENTERS

1. ARGUIM
One of the first European slave trading bases off the coast of Africa, established in 1445.

2. SAO TOME
An island trading base that was a hub for slaves trafficked to the Americas from the Kingdom of Kongo.

3. ELMINA CASTLE
Built in 1482, the slave-holding castle is now the oldest European building south of the Sahara.

4. CANARY ISLANDS
The earliest European demand for African slaves arose from a need for workers in the island colonies of the east Atlantic.

5. HISPANIOLA
The first known African slaves in the Americas arrived in Hispaniola in 1502 after a circuitous passage via Europe.

6. SAN MIGUEL DE GUALDAPE
Founded in 1526 by Lucas Vázquez de Ayllón, the 600 colonists of the first Spanish attempt to colonize the mainland included a number of slaves.

NORTH AMERICA

Slaves were usually captured by fellow African tribes

> "Demand for slaves rocketed after the first explorers returned from the other side of the ocean with tales of unclaimed lands"

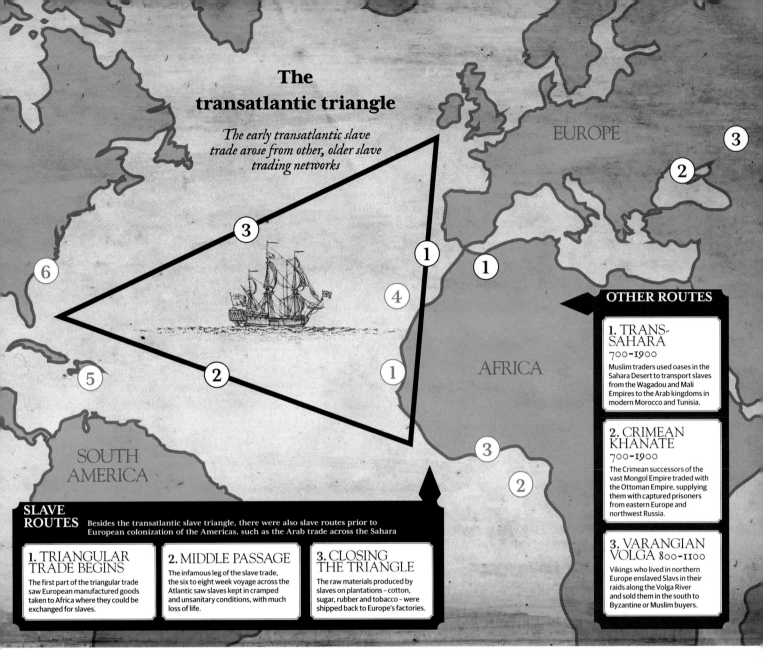

The transatlantic triangle

The early transatlantic slave trade arose from other, older slave trading networks

EUROPE

AFRICA

SOUTH AMERICA

OTHER ROUTES

1. TRANS-SAHARA
700–1900

Muslim traders used oases in the Sahara Desert to transport slaves from the Wagadou and Mali Empires to the Arab kingdoms in modern Morocco and Tunisia.

2. CRIMEAN KHANATE
700–1900

The Crimean successors of the vast Mongol Empire traded with the Ottoman Empire, supplying them with captured prisoners from eastern Europe and northwest Russia.

3. VARANGIAN VOLGA 800–1100

Vikings who lived in northern Europe enslaved Slavs in their raids along the Volga River and sold them in the south to Byzantine or Muslim buyers.

SLAVE ROUTES

Besides the transatlantic slave triangle, there were also slave routes prior to European colonization of the Americas, such as the Arab trade across the Sahara

1. TRIANGULAR TRADE BEGINS

The first part of the triangular trade saw European manufactured goods taken to Africa where they could be exchanged for slaves.

2. MIDDLE PASSAGE

The infamous leg of the slave trade, the six to eight week voyage across the Atlantic saw slaves kept in cramped and unsanitary conditions, with much loss of life.

3. CLOSING THE TRIANGLE

The raw materials produced by slaves on plantations – cotton, sugar, rubber and tobacco – were shipped back to Europe's factories.

---

and female" to "the Indies, the islands, and the mainland of the ocean sea, already discovered or to be discovered" by ship "direct from the isles of Guinea and other regions from which they are wont to bring the said Negroes."

The charter was a reward to de Gorrevod for good service, a chance to make a fortune by granting him the first chance to profit from a new trade route, but he had no intention of involving himself directly in human trafficking. The rights granted to him were subcontracted and resold a number of times until they fell into the hands of a Genoese merchant, Domingo de Fornari; two Castilian merchants, Juan de la Torre and Juan Fernandez de Castro, and a Seville-based Genoese banker, Gaspar Centurion. They arranged for various seafarers to carry out the work of transporting 4,000 African slaves from one side of the Atlantic to the other. At least four voyages took place, in 1519, 1520 – the voyage under the command of Francisco de Rosa – May 1521 and October 1521. Each departed from

Arguim and landed in Puerto Rico, although it is likely that other ships carried slaves from Arguim to Hispaniola. There were also at least six slave voyages from Cape Verde to the Caribbean between 1518 and 1530.

By 1522 direct slave voyages had begun from another starting point: the island of São Tomé some 2,000 miles along the African coast, opposite what is now Gabon. Among these voyages was a ship carrying 139 slaves that voyaged across the Atlantic in 1522, and another with as many as 248 in 1529. The first enslaved Africans to reach mainland North America arrived in 1526 as part of an ill-fated Spanish attempt to colonize San Miguel de Gualdape, while African burials at a cemetery in Campeche, Mexico, suggest that African slaves may have been shipped to Central America almost as soon as Hernán Cortés had subjugated the Aztec and Mayan empires.

The transatlantic slave trade was born. From relatively humble beginnings, the number of

slaves crossing the ocean would grow and grow. British slave ships would soon eclipse the deeds of their Iberian predecessors, transporting millions of slaves in the 18th century.

The scars of the slave trade still remain today. While slave labor in the colonies helped European powers to become rich, industrial nations, the African population and economy stagnated and fell behind the rest of the world. Ever-increasing European demands meant that slave-trading African rulers needed to have a growing, ready supply of slave labor, triggering raids and wars that unsettled the continent and left a legacy of tribal conflict and civil wars. An African diaspora exists throughout North and South America, but long-held racial prejudices have simmered well beyond the end of the slave trade and into the 21st century, especially in the United States. The ill effects of the 400-year transatlantic slave trade were unintended consequences of the Age of Discovery.

THE JAMESTOWN CAPTIVES OF 1619

Discover how the unexpected arrival of enslaved Africans sheds light on the early years of colonial slavery

Written by Scott Reeves

THE JAMESTOWN CAPTIVES OF 1619

The landing of African captives in Virginia was a milestone in the African-American story and North American slavery

Image: Getty Images

I t was probably hot and swelteringly humid, a typical summer day on the mid-Atlantic seaboard, when the ship sailed into Port Comfort and dropped anchor in the James River in late August 1619. Although flying a Dutch flag, the privateer, carrying a letter of marque allowing it to attack Spanish and Portuguese traders, was undeniably English. It had an English name, White Lion, was owned by Robert Rich, the Earl of Warwick, and sailed under a Cornish captain. Their destination was Jamestown in Virginia, the colony's biggest and most important settlement.

The ship's visit was recorded by John Rolfe, a colonist better known to history as the husband of Pocahontas, the Native American princess who

had died two years before in 1617. Rolfe noted that John Jope, the captain of the White Lion, "brought not anything but 20 and odd Negroes, which the Governor and Cape Merchant bought for victuals (whereof he was in great need as he pretended) at the best and easiest rates they could."

It is the traditional starting point of the African-American story, repeated in countless school textbooks and learned by generations of American children. Yet the truth is more nuanced. Although 1619 is often considered to mark the beginning of Black history and American slavery in popular culture, the landing of "20 and odd Negroes" at Jamestown was just one step – albeit an extremely important one – in the surprisingly lengthy creation of North

America's infamous slave system.

It is certainly true that the Africans transported across the Atlantic were taken against their will. The Kimbundu-speaking people from the kingdom of Ndongo, between the Lukala and Kwanza rivers in present-day Angola, lived in a developed urban civilization based around tribally governed towns and villages. The king lived in the capital city, Kabasa, along with 50,000 of his subjects. However, the numerically superior Ndongo were unable to resist when the Portuguese, who had been slowly encroaching into West Africa, allied with an enemy tribe. A military campaign beginning in 1618 drove deep into Ndongo territory and saw thousands of captives marched several hundred miles to the coast. There they boarded at least

36 Iberian slave ships, one of which was the Portuguese vessel São João Bautista, sometimes Hispanicized as San Juan Bautista.

The Atlantic voyage took a heavy toll on its human cargo. Of 350 Africans aboard São João Bautista, around 150 died on its long journey. Then, when the ship was in the relative safety of the Bay of Campeche in the Gulf of Mexico and almost within sight of its destination, Veracruz, it was ambushed by the White Lion and another privateer, the Treasurer. The lumbering slaver was swiftly boarded and, although the English had been hoping for a rich cargo of gold, they made do with around 50 of the remaining Africans instead. São João Bautista limped onwards to Veracruz; the privateers set sail for the new English colony in Virginia but became separated in the choppy waters of the Atlantic.

Governor Sir George Yeardley and head merchant Abraham Piersey may have been surprised by the cargo on offer when the White Lion dropped anchor at Jamestown, but they nonetheless acquired the majority of the 30 or so captives that the ship carried. Four days later, the Treasurer received a less warm welcome at the nearby village of Kikotan. The captain, Daniel Elfrith, had been blamed for an outbreak of dysentery that struck Virginia after his ship had docked the previous year. Elfrith swiftly offloaded a few more captives in exchange for much-needed supplies before the two privateers left and the remaining Africans on board were taken to work on the estates of the Earl of Warwick in Bermuda.

The Africans aboard the White Lion had been ripped from their homeland, forced into a treacherous voyage across the ocean, and survived a battle at sea. Now they found themselves living in a new colony built on a swampy and isolated island in the James River. Established in 1607, Jamestown was hardly the thriving settlement its London investors had hoped for. Native Americans considered the island uninhabitable. That only 60 of 500 colonists managed to survive the first three years indicates they were correct. Evidence suggests that the survivors may have turned to cannibalism during the hungry winter of 1609-10; additional threats came in the forms of disease – hardly surprising given the mosquito-ridden swamps – and the strained relations with the Powhatan Confederacy that occasionally erupted into violent raids.

Yet within a few years, the colonists had successfully established a foothold in the New World. John Rolfe arrived on the third supply fleet from London in 1609 with a bag of tobacco seeds he had obtained from Spanish sources and discovered that Virginia's soil was ideal for tobacco cultivation. The struggling colony had found a profitable trade and it quickly expanded as new land was claimed and planted, often

The bound captives from the White Lion and Treasurer were forced across the Atlantic against their will

The cultivation of tobacco involved hard, manual graft

The first African in North America, a conquistador fighting with Juan Ponce de León, pre-dated the Jamestown captives by more than a century

The invasion of Ndongo

How did Jamestown's first Africans end up aboard a Portuguese slave ship?

Some 101 years before the Ndongo captives arrived in Jamestown, King Manuel I of Portugal received an embassy from his counterpart in the Kingdom of Ndongo, Ngola Kiluanji Kia Samba. The African ruler sought independence from the Kingdom of Kongo, to which Ndongo was a vassal state, and asked for Christian missionaries in the hope that he might forge an alliance with the Europeans. However, it began an uneasy relationship between the two countries that culminated in the Ndongo people being shipped across the Atlantic.

For the next century, the Portuguese began to increase their influence in Kongo and Ndongo, gradually incorporating coastal lands into the colony of Angola and meddling in and disrupting African affairs whenever possible. When the Portuguese came into contact with the Imbangala, a rootless group of nomadic raiders, they encouraged them into the service of the Portuguese king. Thanks to the help of the mercenary bands, Governor Luis Mendes de Vasconcellos was able to invade Ndongo in 1618. The capital was sacked and King Ngola Mbandi was forced to flee to the island of Kindonga in the Kwanza River.

The Ndongo survived the onslaught and peace negotiations brought the war to a close in 1621, but not before thousands of Ndongo subjects had been taken prisoner by the advancing Imbangala. Among them were the 20 or so captives who were marched to the coast and forced aboard the São João Bautista. The next time they stepped on land, it was on the other side of the Atlantic in Jamestown.

Slaves were not usually captured by European traders but were obtained when Africans sold prisoners from other tribes and ethnic groups

---

incurring the wrath of the local native tribes who considered it their own. Hundreds of prospective colonists made the expensive voyage across the Atlantic as indentured servants. In exchange for passage, shelter and food, immigrants agreed to work for planters for three to seven years. They were promised money or a plot of land to make a start as independent workers when their term of service was complete.

The African captives aboard the White Lion would have also been a useful addition to the workforce on tobacco plantations. The names they went by in Africa, even their exact homeland and language, are unknown to

us. Many early colonial census records and documents list Africans only by their race rather than by name; the few who have made a mark in the records are referred to by the Portuguese or English names they were given on board the São João Bautista or in Jamestown.

In a census conducted in March 1620, a few months after the White Lion and Treasurer stopped at Jamestown, there were 32 Africans documented as living in Virginia of whom 15 were men and 17 were women. By 1624, this small African population had shrunk to only 21. Although such a high death rate seems horrifying, it was probably no worse than that

> ## "Many early colonial census records and documents list Africans only by their race rather than by name"

John Rolfe's discovery that Virginia's soil was ideal for growing tobacco gave the colony its first profitable crop

Moroccan Estevanico was one of only four survivors of the doomed 1526 San Miguel de Gualdape expedition

faced by their White contemporaries. Colonists of all races had to face constant outbreaks of illness and disease, while a single attack by the Powhatan tribes in 1622 killed a quarter of the population of the colony in one day.

Only the briefest of details survive about the fragile lives of the Africans. One of the captives who arrived in 1619 was a female named Angelo or Angela. In 1625 she was listed as "Angelo, a Negro woman in the Treasurer," living in the house of Lieutenant William Peirce in Jamestown, probably sharing domestic duties with three White indentured servants. In 2017, archaeologists at Jamestown uncovered a cowrie shell at the site of Peirce's house. Cowrie shells were valuable artifacts in West Africa, used as currency and in religious practices, and it was likely an object of special significance to his African servant.

Two Africans by the names of Anthony and Isabella married and lived in Elizabeth City, just outside Jamestown, where they worked for Captain William Tucker, a Virginia Company of London stockholder. In 1624, Anthony and

Isabella had a son they named William Tucker after their employer. The baby was the first person of African ancestry born in the English colonies of North America.

Yet, unlike countless Black babies born in the colonies and the United States over the next two centuries, William Tucker was not born a slave. The Africans who disembarked the White Lion and Treasurer worked under contract as indentured servants rather than as slaves. Virginia's General Assembly had seen no need to legislate slavery into the laws of the colony and, as a consequence, the Africans were bound by the same rights, duties, privileges and punishments as White migrants who accepted terms of indentured servitude. Although they were probably given no choice but to accept the terms of service, the African captives who completed their contracts were granted 25 to 50 acres to grow their own tobacco or other crops and some basic supplies to get them through their first year as a free laborer. There's no denying that indentured service was a harsh,

backbreaking life with restrictions on civil liberties.

Some Africans took advantage of this early equity in the law to rise up in society. Like most of the other early Africans in North America, we do not know the name that Anthony Johnson was born with in West Africa. He sailed to Jamestown from London in 1621 aboard the James. After working for several years on the tobacco plantation belonging to wealthy merchant Edward Bennett, he was released from his contract of servitude sometime after 1635. Johnson began his life as a free man alongside his wife, Mary, another African who was shipped to Jamestown to work on Bennett's plantation in 1623. He set to work building up his own small-scale tobacco plantation, including taking on his own indentured servants, both Black and White.

Nevertheless, although they benefitted from far more equality than in subsequent decades and centuries, the first Africans in Jamestown almost certainly suffered racial discrimination. There was already an established racial caste

The first African-American family

Is a small burial ground in Hampton the last resting place of some Jamestown captives?

Tucker's Cemetery claims to be the oldest African-American burial ground in the USA

Although only fragments of documents survive to piece together the lives of Jamestown's first Africans, it is possible their mortal remains are still with us. Tucker's Cemetery in Hampton has been used for generations of Black Virginians, some of whom believe oral histories trace their ancestors back to William Tucker – the first baby of African descent born in Virginia – and beyond to Angola.

Although tombstones and records of burials only date back to the 1800s, a ground-penetrating radar survey of the two-acre site, once known as the Old Colored Burial Ground, has found another 104 unmarked burials that may date to the 17th and 18th centuries. A macabre discovery was made in July 2017, when a keen groundskeeper cut back some out-of-control shrubbery. He found the roots

had displaced a skull from an old grave; experts concluded that it belonged to an approximately 60-year-old female of African ancestry.

Since the cemetery is only 400 meters from the site of William Tucker's plantation, it is a fascinating possibility that one of the graves may even belong to William Tucker himself, although chances of identifying it are almost zero since we know nothing of the firstborn African American beyond the fact that he was born and baptized. After that, he disappears into the mists of history. Did he survive childhood and did he have his own children who became the modern Virginians who claim him as an ancestor today? And, given how the status of Black Africans was changing in Virginia's early years, did Tucker end his life as a free man, a servant or a slave?

Archaeologists have uncovered the Virginia house in which Treasurer captive Angela lived

system in the Portuguese and Spanish colonies of the New World, and it is likely that the English colonists viewed their Black counterparts with a degree of prejudice, too. As the years passed, laws were drawn up that condemned some Black workers to be indentured for life and codified the institution of slavery.

> ## "Punch was a servant for life or, to put it another way, a slave with no chance of freedom"

The first definitive instance of lifetime servitude was recorded in July 1640 by Virginia's General Court. John Punch, a Black indentured servant, escaped from his master, Hugh Gwyn, along with two White servants. After capture, the courts extended the indenture contracts of the Dutch and Scottish runaways by four years. Punch received a much harsher sentence: "the third being a Negro named John Punch shall serve his said master or his assigns for the time of his natural life here or elsewhere." Essentially, Punch was now a servant for life or, to put it another way, a slave with no chance of earning his freedom.

Even Black people could become slave owners under the new system. In 1653, Anthony Johnson – the African who had worked his way to freedom under the terms of his indentured servitude – was taken to court by one of his Black workers, John Casor, who claimed his indenture had expired seven years earlier and that he was being held illegally by Johnson. Casor won his freedom after a legal battle and went to work for a different planter, but the appeals court reversed the decision and ruled that Casor did not have proof that he had a contract of indenture. Essentially, the judiciary determined that Casor was not an indentured servant but a slave who was required to work for Johnson for the rest of his life.

While the cases of John Punch and John Casor gave judicial sanction to the idea of lifetime servitude, a 1662 law extended the institution of slavery. It was a direct response to a 1660 legal challenge by Elizabeth Key. A Virginia-born daughter of an African servant and an English planter, Key argued that she was not a slave but a free woman due to her White English father. Although she won her battle for freedom, the Virginia legislature ensured that similar claims in future would fail when they passed a law stating that all children born in the colony would take the status of their mothers, regardless of paternity. Since Black women were far more likely to have a child to White men than Black men were to have a child with a White woman, due to the fact that many slaves were abused by their owners, the new law was a deliberately racist policy. Children born to enslaved mothers would be enslaved themselves; slavery was no longer limited to a Black woman's lifetime but extended to their offspring, too.

The status of African Americans in the English colonies was confirmed. Slavery was codified. Yet it took more than 40 years from the landing of the White Lion at Port Comfort to establish the institution of slavery. The Jamestown captives of 1619 and their immediate successors – though forcibly removed from their homeland and having to endure terrible hardships – were still given opportunities and liberties that would have seemed unimaginable to the generations who followed.

Just as the disembarkation of the handful of Ndongo in 1619 did not mark the beginning of slavery in North America, their arrival was not the starting point of African-American history as a whole. Around half a million Africans are thought to have crossed the Atlantic in the century or so prior to the arrival of the Jamestown captives. As early as the voyages of Christopher Columbus, Black Africans were transported from one side of the Atlantic Ocean to the other. The exact status of Columbus's Africans – whether they were slaves or free – is unclear. What we do know is that there was already an established system of Africans being enslaved and put to work in Europe or in the first European colonies on the islands off Africa. As early as 1501, slaves crossed the Atlantic as Portugal and Spain began building up their young colonies in Brazil and Uruguay on the back of slave labor.

In 1513, the first documented case of an African stepping on North American soil was recorded. Juan Garrido was not a slave but a soldier, born in Kongo but fighting for the King of Spain. After participating in the conquests of Hispaniola, Puerto Rico and Cuba, Garrido joined the expedition of Juan Ponce de León that searched for the Fountain of Youth in present-day Florida. Garrido's time in North America was limited. By 1520 he was part of the army besieging the Aztec capital Tenochtitlan and he retired to a farm in Mexico City.

While Garrido went on to spend his old age tending crops in his fields, the Spanish effort to colonize North America continued. In 1526, an expedition on behalf of Emperor Charles I attempted to settle in San Miguel de Gualdape on the Georgian coast. It was an ill-fated venture, doomed to failure due to starvation, disease, and hostile Native Americans – a disastrous triumvirate of threats that would become familiar to colonial ventures over the next century – but the final nail in the coffin was a

Francis Drake hoped to add African slaves to Roanoke's workforce in 1586 but ended up evacuating the colony to England

"Children born to enslaved mothers would be enslaved themselves; slavery was no longer limited to a Black woman's lifetime"

slave rebellion. The exact number of slaves in the colony is unknown, the only contemporary chronicle merely states that "some" of the 600 settlers were Black Africans. The same account notes that the slaves "had their reasons" for burning down the house of one of the colony's leaders, and some historians suggest that the slaves managed to escape to live among the local native tribes.

Whatever the fate of the San Miguel de Gualdape slaves, it is clear that captive Africans were part of the expedition and, despite the revolt, slaves continued to be shipped to the Spanish New World. In 1528, the Narváez Expedition left Cuba and landed in Florida (although they were actually aiming for Mexico)

The new colony of Jamestown was only 12 years old when the first Africans arrived

Within three years of landing in Virginia, the African captives faced a massacre by the Powhatan that killed a quarter of the colony's population

W 96
FIRST AFRICANS IN VIRGINIA

The first documented Africans in Virginia arrived in 1619 when a Dutch warship landed here at Point Comfort. The "twenty and odd" Africans, captured from the Spanish, were traded to the Virginia colonists in exchange for foodstuffs. Early Africans who lived here included Antony and Isabell, and their son William, likely the first black child in present-day Hampton. They served Point Comfort Commander William Tucker, but whether the early Africans were treated as indentured servants or slaves is uncertain. The institution of slavery evolved during the 17th century as the term of service for Africans was extended for life. The U.S. abolished slavery in 1865.

The exact place the White Lion dropped anchor is now part of Fort Monroe National Monument

The journey of African captives to Jamestown in 1619 was a vital step on the path to creating the notorious slave system in North America

with the aim of founding two new towns. It was another almighty failure that only ended eight years later when four survivors from the original pioneers trekked into Mexico City, having been forced into a slow cross-continental journey around the Gulf of Mexico. One of the four was Andrés Dorantes de Carranza, who was accompanied by his Moroccan slave, Estevanico. The African's reward for accompanying his master and surviving against all odds was not freedom. Instead he was sold to the Viceroy of New Spain and tasked with leading further expeditions into North America. The three White survivors politely declined similar offers; Estevanico had no choice.

It was not just the Spanish who included slaves in their difficult attempts to settle in North America. Enslaved Africans may have been on board Sir Francis Drake's fleet when he arrived at Roanoke Island in 1586. The famed English privateer had plundered the Spanish settlements at Cartagena on the coast of Colombia and St

Augustine in Florida, making off with both Native American and African slaves who he intended to disembark in the Virginian colony. He expected to find a flourishing settlement in need of labor; he actually found a starving population begging him to return them to England. Drake took them home but it appears few slaves accompanied the failed colonists on the voyage to Europe, whether they were sold in the Caribbean en route or simply abandoned in the New World is unknown. Perhaps the saddest part of the story is that nobody bothered to record what happened to them.

Drake was already familiar with the slave trade prior to his journey to Roanoke. In the 1560s, he and his cousin, John Hawkins, were part of three voyages to Guinea and Sierra Leone, capturing more than 1,000 Africans from Portuguese bases and transporting them to Spanish planters in Hispaniola. These crossings were among the first that English seafarers made in the slave trade. Fifty years later, when English colonies

were established on the islands of the Atlantic, slaves followed. In 1612, Bermuda was the focus of a settlement party. Within four years, enslaved Africans were taken from former Spanish colonies in the Caribbean to Bermuda, pre-dating the arrival of the Jamestown captives by three years.

The English were not the first to transport Africans across the Atlantic, nor were the Jamestown captives the first Africans to set foot in the colonies of the New World. Angela, Anthony, Isabella, and their contemporaries who disembarked at Jamestown were taken against their will, but they were not slaves in the same way that millions of others of their race would be in North America. However, the landing of the White Lion in 1619 was an important milestone in African-American history; a key step in the long journey that culminated in the most notorious and infamous example of chattel slavery based on race.

ENSLAVED BY THE PRESIDENT

George Washington, the first president of the United States, watches over enslaved Black laborers at his Mount Vernon estate. Like many of the Founding Fathers and early presidents of the United States, Washington was a slave owner. At the time of his death in 1799, the enslaved population of his estate was 317. Although many of the Founding Fathers acknowledged that slavery violated the core American Revolutionary ideal of liberty, it would take a bloody Civil War before the horrors of slavery were finally outlawed in the US.

SLAVERY IN NORTH AMERICA

Slavery was not the foundation of America but it was there not long after the beginning and all but tore the country apart – the rift culminating in a bloody civil war

Written by Edoardo Albert

Far from slavery being peculiar to North America, it is an almost universal human institution throughout recorded history, accepted by some as the natural order of things. Only in the civilizations deriving from Christianity and Buddhism was slavery frowned upon, and even so the practice went on, albeit in reduced numbers. However, as Europeans ventured upon their Age of Discovery from the late 15th century onwards, they resumed the practice of slave trading, aided by the incessant internal wars in Africa that produced local chiefs eager and willing to sell prisoners of war to European traders. The trade network in African slaves predated the arrival of Europeans, with much of it having been directed towards feeding the demand from Muslim rulers for African slaves, however the caravels and galleons that anchored off the west coast of Africa provided a new and lucrative export market. European merchants, eager to feed the exploding taste for sugar, started shipping increasing numbers of slaves to the Caribbean sugar plantations. Having offloaded their cargo of slaves, the ships loaded with sugar and returned to Europe, creating the triangular trade network – Europe, Africa, America – that drove the Atlantic slave trade. At its peak, this shipment of people across the sea became a vast enterprise, transporting millions of souls into a life of bondage, before the contradictions at its core produced the movement that finally brought it to an end. But while it existed, the Atlantic slave trade was a conveyor belt of suffering and injustice, of moral hypocrisy and the degrading effects of power.

NOTICE

NEGROES
FOR SALE
AT AUCTION
TH'S DAY
AT 1 O'CLOCK.

THE NEW YORK HERALD

An illustration of a slave auction in Virginia, 1861

Historians currently estimate that between 12 and 12.8 million Africans were transported during the Atlantic slave trade, a conveyor belt of human misery

A female convict, transported from an English prison to Jamestown, Virginia, as an indentured servant is sold for a wife to a male settler for 100 pounds of tobacco

THE COLONIAL ERA

What would become the United States of America was not a draw for European emigrants in the early decades of the 17th century. Those seeking their fortunes were much more likely to head for the Caribbean islands, with their sugar plantations, or to South America with its gold and silver. It was so hard to attract settlers to North America that the early colonists started importing people. The first shipload of Black African slaves arrived in 1619 in Jamestown to work in the labor-intensive tobacco fields that were starting to produce an economically viable crop for the young colony. These Black Africans found themselves laboring alongside poor White Europeans who were there before them and who shared the same unfree status.

THE WHITE LABOR TRADE

The British colony in Jamestown, Virginia, was no New World paradise but a harsh and unforgiving place, requiring backbreaking labor in its fields and with high rates of mortality among its inhabitants. To provide a workforce and a future for the colony, poor White Europeans – mainly from England, Wales, Scotland and Ireland, although some came from the Netherlands and other countries in Europe – were recruited. Their passages to the New World were paid at the price of their freedom: they became indentured laborers, which essentially meant they were time-limited slaves, tied to their employer and not free to marry or work for themselves until they had worked out the terms of their contract, and paid back the cost of their passage. Over half the Europeans who came to North America before the Revolution came as indentured servants. It was a hard and precarious existence, its misery made explicit by the letters that young Richard Frethorne wrote home in March 1623, begging that his indenture be paid off or food sent over, for he was ill from lack of food and the bloody flux, while back home beggars were given more than he received as his daily ration. Frethorne was probably 12 when he arrived in America. His letters never reached his parents, staying in the offices of the Virginia Company in London, and Frethorne himself was dead by February 1624, probably not yet 15.

"It was so hard to attract settlers to North America that the early colonists started importing people"

In the early decades of the 17th century, Black slaves were not particularly differentiated from White indentured laborers, constituting only about five percent of the population and sharing the possibility of working towards freedom. Anthony Johnson, who was brought to Jamestown in 1621, was nevertheless allowed to work land for himself by his owner. Around 1641 Johnson was granted his freedom and in 1650, he was allotted 250 acres of land as his own, and his sons were granted equivalent amounts of land. Johnson became successful; so successful that he acquired his own slaves. There were some other free Blacks in and around Jamestown but by 1650, most Black people were slaves. It had taken Johnson 20 years of work to reclaim his freedom; White indentured laborers generally earned it back after seven years work. The barriers between the races were going up.

Further north, in the Dutch-owned colony of New Amsterdam, which would later be

The first Black slaves arrived in Jamestown in 1619, taken from a Portuguese ship that had been captured by a British privateer

An idealized version of the signing of the US Constitution painted in 1940 by Howard Chandler Christy

Three-fifths of all other persons

A key question faced by the Constitutional Convention summoned to establish how the new United States of America would be governed was how many delegates each state would have in the House of Representatives, and how much tax each state would pay. The interests of the Northern and Southern states had already diverged and there was a real possibility that the United States would break up before it properly came into existence. As such, the delegates to the convention tried to find a way to tie in the Southern, slave-owning states to the Northern states, where slavery was gradually being abolished. The compromise came in the method of calculating the population of each state, whereby the number of delegates to Congress would be apportioned. The Northern states had significantly higher populations of freemen than the Southern states. However, if the slave populations of the Southern states were included in their count, that would even out the numbers significantly. But slaves had no voting or other rights, and in the Southern states were regarded in law as property, not people. Nevertheless, the delegates to the Constitution agreed a compromise where a slave was regarded as three-fifths a freeman for the purpose of sending delegates to Congress. Up until the outbreak of the American Civil War, the Three-Fifths Compromise effectively handed the Southern slave states greater political power than they would have otherwise had.

renamed New York, the Dutch West India Company imported 11 African slaves along with its settlers, and later brought in Black women as wives for these men. The company proved vital in the frequent disputes with the local Native Americans and it armed the Black slaves to help in the defense of the colony. Knowing themselves a vital part of the colony's defenses, the Black slaves negotiated a settlement with the Dutch West India Company that constituted a sort of half-freedom, where they continued to be slaves of the company but were free to work in their own regard when they were not required elsewhere.

The Puritan colony in Massachusetts lived by a conviction of divinely ordained social strata with the Pauline injunction to treat slaves as brothers, which somehow managed to combine charity and condescension in a particularly hypocritical mixture. However, Black slaves never came to form a large part of the population in Massachusetts – Native Americans were captured and enslaved in larger numbers in Massachusetts and New Amsterdam/York, with a vigorous trade down to Virginia and South Carolina. The trade in Native Americans was facilitated by tribes selling captured enemies for profit – just as was happening across the Atlantic in Africa. However, Native Americans proved more problematic as slaves. Because they were familiar with the land, and with relatives and friends often close at hand, it was far easier for enslaved Native Americans to escape their slavery, or for their family to rescue them, sometimes with fatal consequences for the slave owner. So grave did these reprisals become that in 1679, New York outlawed the enslavement of local Native Americans and in 1706, it forbade the enslavement of any Native Americans. The statute stipulated that "Negroes alone shall be slaves."

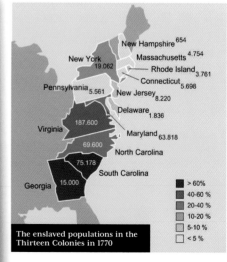

A handbill advertising the sale of slaves in Charleston, South Carolina, in 1769

TO BE SOLD,

On THURSDAY the third Day
of AUGUST next,

A CARGO

OF

NINETY-FOUR

PRIME, HEALTHY

NEGROES,

CONSISTING OF

Thirty-nine MEN, Fifteen BOYS,
Twenty-four WOMEN, and
Sixteen GIRLS.

JUST ARRIVED,

In the Brigantine DEMBIA, *Francis Bare*, Mafter, from SIERRA-
LEON, by

DAVID & JOHN DEAS.

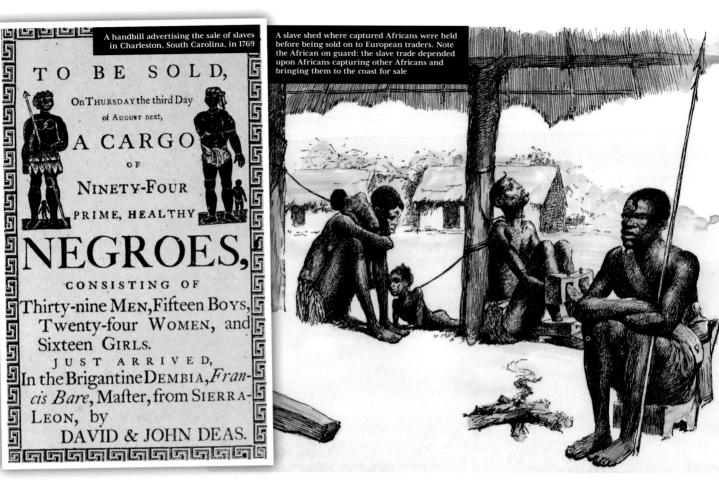

A slave shed where captured Africans were held before being sold on to European traders. Note the African on guard: the slave trade depended upon Africans capturing other Africans and bringing them to the coast for sale

THE CODIFICATION OF SLAVERY

For the first half of the 17th century, there was little legal basis for slavery as a race-based system of perpetual servitude. However, in the second half of the century, a series of laws and court decisions laid the legal basis for the institution of slavery in North America. A foretaste came in 1640 via a ruling by a Virginia court on three runaway indentured servants. All three servants were whipped, with the two White servants being ordered to labor an extra year for their master and three further years for the colony. However the third servant, a Black man named John Punch, was condemned to "serve his said master or his assigns for the time of his natural life." The Virginia court explicitly said that it reached this decision because John Punch was Black.

Virginia, Maryland, New York, Connecticut, and South Carolina all enacted statutes establishing and regulating slavery in the second half of the 17th century. In a 1662 law, Virginia declared that slavery was hereditary and matrilineal: you were a slave if your mother was a slave. This made slavery easier to regulate, as it was much more straightforward to determine the mother of a child than the father. It also codified the extensive sexual slavery taking place in the colony, where White masters impregnated their Black female slaves, enabling them to claim their own children as their slaves.

Virginia also moved to close the religion loophole: although Christians had long demurred at the idea of enslaving other Christians, the colony resolved in law that slaves remained slaves even if they were baptized Christians. Color was coming to trump faith. Continuing to lead the way in the codification of the laws of slavery, in 1669 Virginia also enacted a statute declaring that an owner killing his slave through enthusiastic punishment would not be guilty of murder. After all, the slave was his property. A slave owner wouldn't wilfully destroy his own property so there could be no intention to kill.

Where slavery in early colonial America was based upon class, the growth of legislation in the second half of the 17th century shows its

A colonial American soapmaker being assisted by his indentured servant in his work

The enslaved populations in the Thirteen Colonies in 1770

New Hampshire 654
New York 19.062
Massachusetts 4.754
Rhode Island 3.761
Connecticut 5.698
Pennsylvania 5.561
New Jersey 8.220
Delaware 1.836
Virginia 187.600
Maryland 63.818
North Carolina 69.600
South Carolina 75.178
Georgia 15.000

> 60%
40-60 %
20-40 %
10-20 %
5-10 %
< 5 %

The Dred Scott ruling

Dred and Harriet Scott, whose quest for freedom resulted in the American Civil War

In 1836, Dr John Emerson, a surgeon serving the United States Army, moved from the slave state of Missouri to the free state of Illinois, taking with him his slave, Dred Scott. In 1840, Emerson returned to Missouri, taking the now married Dred Scott with him. Emerson died in 1843 and his widow, Irene, inherited his estate, including his slaves, Dred and Harriet Scott. In 1846, Scott attempted to purchase freedom for his family, offering Irene Emerson $300. She refused. Scott then took the case to court, arguing that having lived in a free state for three years he and his wife had automatically been freed. The case went all the way to the United States Supreme Court. The issue of slavery was tearing apart the young nation and the justices of the Supreme Court thought that by settling the matter decisively they could bring an end to the debate that was causing so much friction. On March 6, 1857,

the Supreme Court gave a 7-2 majority decision, dismissing the case. Chief Justice Roger Taney wrote a long opinion stating the reasons for the decision, chief among them being that people of African descent "are not included, and were not intended to be included, under the word 'citizens' in the Constitution, and can therefore claim none of the rights and privileges which that instrument provides for and secures to citizens of the United States." The judgement had exactly the opposite effect, inflaming tensions and contributing materially to the descent into civil war. Of all the decisions handed down by the Supreme Court, Dred Scott is universally regarded as the worst. It was abrogated after the Civil War by the Thirteenth and Fourteenth Amendments to the Constitution of the United States. As for Dred Scott, he was manumitted on May 26, 1857 but died from tuberculosis on September 17, 1858.

> ## "Virginia was changing into a slave-based society, where most labor was done by slaves and all the slaves were Black"

mutation into an explicitly racial and racist institution. While the majority of labor was still done by White indentured workers, the new American elite were able to divide opposition to their rule by placing Black slaves at a lower level than the White indentured laborers. A hierarchy was also created among Black slaves, with favored house slaves at the top, then artisans and field laborers – the majority – at

the bottom. A side effect of this hierarchy of slavery was that many planned rebellions and escapes were betrayed by those higher in the hierarchy, anxious at losing their privileged position or through loyalty to an owner who had been kind.

The dependence on slavery for labor increased following Bacon's Rebellion. By 1676 the situation for indentured White servants

was worsening in Virginia, with laws aimed at keeping them from becoming landowners at the end of their period of servitude: the rich, landed class in Virginia was intent on keeping the land for itself. With resentment growing, Nathaniel Bacon, a rich man but the leader of the landless, led a rebellion that saw the governor's house stoned and the capital razed to the ground. However, Bacon died of dysentery, leaving the rebellion leaderless, and reinforcements from England brought it to an end. After the rebellion, the rich and powerful landed elite of Virginia began to invest more in Black slaves, no longer trusting White indentured labor, while the opening up of territory to the west diverted some of the dispossessed by giving them the opportunity to become landowners. In 1680 there were 3,000 Black slaves in Virginia. Forty years later, in 1720, this had grown to 27,000. Virginia was changing into a slave-based society, where most labor was done by slaves and all the slaves were Black. By the end of the 17th century, slavery had been established in all the North American colonies.

SLAVERY IN COLONIAL-ERA AMERICA

From the start, there was a division in the practice of slavery between the northern and southern colonies. The climate and soil of New England did not favor large plantations, so slaves were generally employed in a wide variety of tasks, from household servants to farm workers to artisans, often working alongside their owner. However, in the South, the tobacco plantations that provided the wealth for the landed class were extremely labor intensive. Gangs of Black slaves worked the fields, housed in barracks or shacks, and generally kept apart from the White population. The slave society was becoming increasingly segregated, and a raft of anti-miscegenation laws sought to keep it that way – although the sheer number of laws outlawing sexual relations between the races suggest that such relations occurred far more frequently than the segregationists would have liked.

In order to cement control over their slaves, a series of laws passed in the colonies with the largest slave populations prohibiting teaching Black people how to read and write. South Carolina was the first to enact such legislation, its 1740 Negro Act making it illegal to teach slaves to read or write. However, the first Act proved insufficient and new laws were passed in 1800 and again in 1834, increasing the severity of punishment. That new laws had to be passed demonstrates that enslaved Black people understood perfectly well the worth of learning to read and write, and were willing to risk the punishments enshrined in law in order to do so. The ability to read and write enabled slaves to forge the written passes necessary to travel away from their owner and, more importantly, it opened up the Bible to them. Reading the book that their owners professed to follow revealed the hypocrisy of the slave owners and offered hopes of deliverance and redemption to the slaves themselves. After all, the Biblical narrative of Israel was that of a people delivered from bondage and slavery by God: it takes a slave to fully understand the story of the freeing of an enslaved people from bondage in Egypt.

There were also a few slave revolts, although none on the scale of the slave revolts on some Caribbean islands. The largest pre-Revolution revolt occurred in 1739 in South Carolina, near the Stono River. A literate slave, Jemmy, led 20 men in an attack on a store where they killed the owners and took guns and ammunition. Now armed, the group set off, marching south, heading for Spanish-ruled Florida, where the law stated that slaves who had escaped from the British colonies would be freed. The rebels recruited men as they headed south, as well as killing Whites, before the local militia caught up with them. The rebels lost the battle but the survivors kept heading south, gradually being rounded up and executed by vengeful and fearful Whites.

The largest slave revolt, the Turner Rebellion, started on August 21, 1831 in Virginia, when America was splitting apart into slave and free states. Nat Turner, with between 60 and 80 men, killed 55 Whites before the White militias caught up with them. Turner escaped and remained at large for two months before being captured. Put on trial, Turner was sentenced to death and hung on November 11. After his death, Turner's body was flayed and his skin used for souvenir purses, his flesh boiled down for grease and his bones divided.

SLAVERY DURING REVOLUTION

The Stono and Turner rebellions took place before and after the Revolutionary War (1775-83). The war was framed by its American protagonists as a fight for liberty and, as such, many of the enslaved people of North America adopted the same language to call for their own emancipation. After the colonies became independent from Britain, the resulting settlement, as codified in the American Constitution, ended up dividing the country into free and slave states, a division that eventually led to the American Civil War and the final, bloody end to slavery in North America (although by no means was it the end of segregation or discrimination).

In fact, the first man to die in the American Revolutionary War was Black. Crispus Attucks was living in Boston, Massachusetts, when on March 5, 1770, he joined in with a group of locals involved in a fracas with British troops.

The first person to die in the American Revolutionary War was Crispus Attucks, a Black man, during the skirmish with British troops on March 5, 1770 that became known as the Boston Massacre

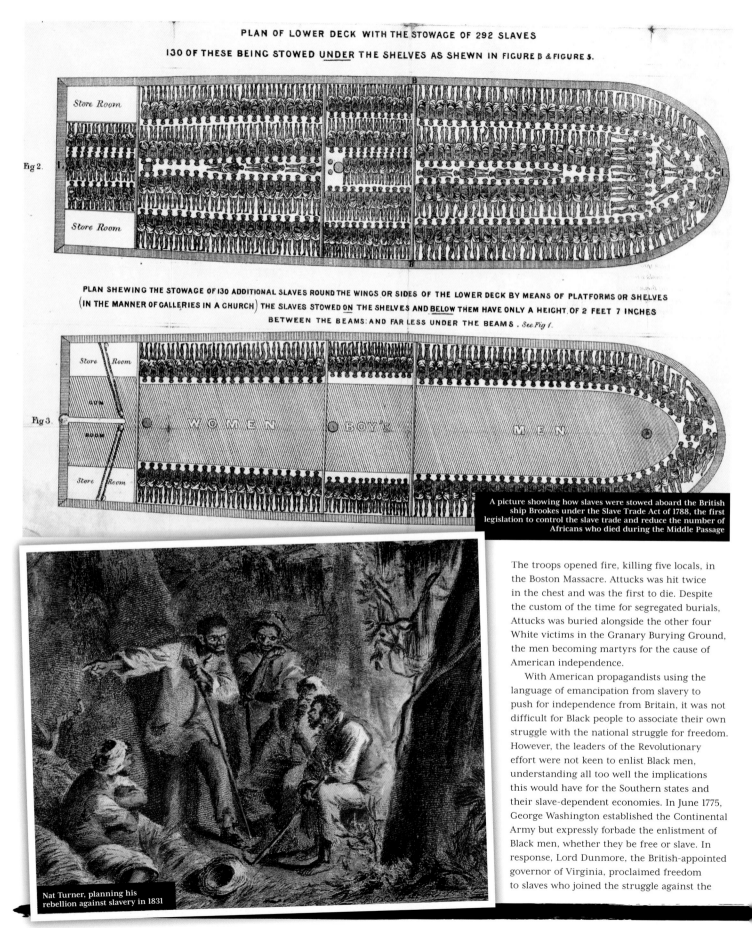

PLAN OF LOWER DECK WITH THE STOWAGE OF 292 SLAVES

130 OF THESE BEING STOWED UNDER THE SHELVES AS SHEWN IN FIGURE B & FIGURE 5.

Fig 2.

Store Room

Store Room

PLAN SHEWING THE STOWAGE OF 130 ADDITIONAL SLAVES ROUND THE WINGS OR SIDES OF THE LOWER DECK BY MEANS OF PLATFORMS OR SHELVES (IN THE MANNER OF GALLERIES IN A CHURCH) THE SLAVES STOWED ON THE SHELVES AND BELOW THEM HAVE ONLY A HEIGHT OF 2 FEET 7 INCHES BETWEEN THE BEAMS: AND FAR LESS UNDER THE BEAMS. See Fig 1.

Fig 3.

Store Room

GUN ROOM

Store Room

WOMEN   BOY'S   MEN

A picture showing how slaves were stowed aboard the British ship Brookes under the Slave Trade Act of 1788, the first legislation to control the slave trade and reduce the number of Africans who died during the Middle Passage

Nat Turner, planning his rebellion against slavery in 1831

The troops opened fire, killing five locals, in the Boston Massacre. Attucks was hit twice in the chest and was the first to die. Despite the custom of the time for segregated burials, Attucks was buried alongside the other four White victims in the Granary Burying Ground, the men becoming martyrs for the cause of American independence.

With American propagandists using the language of emancipation from slavery to push for independence from Britain, it was not difficult for Black people to associate their own struggle with the national struggle for freedom. However, the leaders of the Revolutionary effort were not keen to enlist Black men, understanding all too well the implications this would have for the Southern states and their slave-dependent economies. In June 1775, George Washington established the Continental Army but expressly forbade the enlistment of Black men, whether they be free or slave. In response, Lord Dunmore, the British-appointed governor of Virginia, proclaimed freedom to slaves who joined the struggle against the

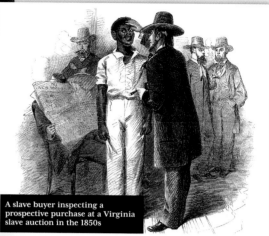

A slave buyer inspecting a prospective purchase at a Virginia slave auction in the 1850s

In 1676, a group of rebels led by Nathaniel Bacon set fire to Jamestown in protest against the governor, William Berkeley. Fear of unrest among indentured servants led to the importation of more Black slaves

"Just as laws had slowly established slavery, they were used in Northern states to outlaw it"

American revolutionaries. Despite the Virginia legislature passing a law that ordered death for any Black man who enlisted with the English, thousands of people made their way to the British camps and were enlisted in the Ethiopian Regiment whose motto was 'Liberty to Slaves'.

Fearing runaway recruitment of slaves by the British, Washington was forced to change tack and allow Black men to enlist in the Continental Army. New York, New Jersey, and Connecticut all allowed slave owners to free slaves to serve in the Continental Army, with the other Northern states following suit. South Carolina, however, never felt the need to extend this possibility to its Black population.

When the British finally lost the war, some 4,000 Black people left the country, sailing under the Royal Navy's protection to their new homes. Meanwhile on the victorious side, 5,000 Black men had fought as part of the Continental Army and the vast majority of these were formally emancipated afterwards, greatly increasing the number of free Black

people in the new nation.

It was not just Black people who could not square the language of liberty that had inspired the Revolution with the reality of slavery. In September 1774, Abigail Adams, the wife of future president John Adams, wrote to him saying, "I wish most sincerely that there was not a slave in the province... It always seemed a most iniquitous scheme to me to fight ourselves for what we are daily robbing and plundering from those who have as good a right to freedom as we have." Indeed, of the first 12 presidents of the United States, only John Adams and his son, John Quincy Adams, never personally owned any slaves.

The Adams were by no means alone in their repugnance of slavery and following American independence, the Northern states gradually moved to outlaw slavery. Just as laws had slowly established slavery, so they were now used in Northern states to outlaw it. In line with the new constitution of Massachusetts, its courts declared slavery "effectively abolished." By 1790, there were no slaves in the state. Emancipation

proceeded more slowly in the other Northern states, with the last slave freed in New York in 1827, but in the North it was a one-way street towards freedom.

However, the question was far from settled in the Southern states. The Constitutional Convention that met in 1787 to formulate the government for the new country was faced with conflicting wishes from the delegates representing the 13 states. To hold the country together, its new Constitution, while never using the word 'slavery', nevertheless tacitly allowed it while also deciding when Congress would be free to pass a law outlawing the slave trade across the Atlantic. The Constitution also made provision for escaped slaves to be returned to their owners.

At the convention, the delegates from Georgia, South Carolina, and North Carolina threatened to walk out if the importation of slaves was outlawed, even though the other ten states had already outlawed the importation of new slaves from Africa. South Carolina delegate Charles Pinckney stated that "South Carolina and Georgia cannot do without slaves." The Convention therefore decided that Congress would only be able to ban the Atlantic trade for 20 years. South Carolina imported 40,000 slaves before the trade was outlawed in 1808. The Constitution, in Article 4, section 2, also provided for the return of escaped slaves to their owners.

Overall the rhetoric and logic of the

The Royal African Company

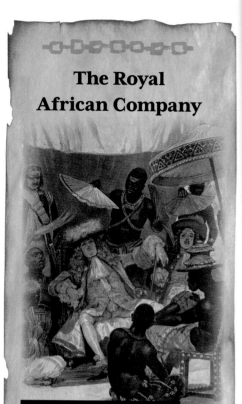

An officer of the Royal African Company concluding a treaty with a Gold Coast king for the trade of slaves

The North Atlantic slave trade was done for money. Greed, pure and simple greed was its driver and nowhere was that greed exhibited more purely or more brutally than by the Royal African Company. The company was incorporated in 1660 by King Charles II, his brother James, Duke of York, and merchants of the City of London and was first called the Company of Royal Adventurers Trading into Africa. If this sounds romantic, it was: the original intention was to search for gold. However, gold proved hard to find and a new charter in 1863 was expanded to include the trade in slaves. At this time, European nations maintained forts on the coast of Africa but depended upon local African rulers to bring slaves in for trade. The first company was rendered insolvent by losses incurred during the Second Anglo-Dutch War and was supplanted in 1672 by the Royal African Company with a broader remit and more powers, including the right to found forts and institute martial law in pursuit of profit, whether that be by gold, trade or slavery. Working with local African rulers, the Royal African Company began transporting large numbers of slaves across the Atlantic, most going to the Caribbean islands but some continuing to North America. The Company transported 5,000 slaves a year, with estimates suggesting that 20 percent died en route. In 1698, Parliament abolished the monopoly the Royal African Company had on the Atlantic slave trade. Faced with competition, the company went bust in 1708, although it continued trading in a reduced manner until 1752.

An enslaved Black family working on a plantation

Constitution greatly strengthened the case for the emancipation of slaves, with the institution disappearing entirely in the Northern states. Perhaps the same logic might have worked, albeit more gradually, in the Southern states, if not for the invention of the cotton gin. Tobacco was an intensive crop that exhausted the soil; so a new harvest was needed to maintain the economic base of the Southern, agricultural states. That crop was cotton. But it was Eli Whitney's invention in 1793 of the cotton gin, a machine for quickly and efficiently separating cotton fibers from seeds, that made cotton big business. The Southern plantations switched to growing cotton and, with demand burgeoning, the plantation owners grew richer than ever. Cotton, like tobacco, was labor intensive and the Southern plantation owners, as well as their political sponsors, saw slavery as the foundation of their wealth and their position. In response to the abolition movement, Southern writers began to actively promote slavery as a social and moral good. The contest might have continued, locked into a stalemate between the Northern and Southern states, if it were not for the western expansion of the United States. As America grew, the question of the status of the new states and territories it was incorporating, became more and more pressing. Both sides correctly believed that the soul of the new nation was at stake.

WEST TO CIVIL WAR

At the start of the 19th century, America was divided about slavery. But the Union had been preserved by the division being equal. Half the 22 states comprising the United States were free states and half were slave states. But when Missouri petitioned to join the Union as a slave state, that delicate balance came under threat.

When Missouri passed the population threshold it applied for admittance to the United States. As a new state, it would be entitled to two senators in the Senate, thus upsetting the balance between free and slave states. As rancour grew between the opposing sides, Henry Clay, the speaker of the House of Representatives, brokered a compromise whereby Missouri entered the Union as a slave state but, at the same time, so did Maine as a free state. Thus the balance would be maintained. But, critically, the bill as passed also decreed that slavery should not be allowed north of the line of latitude at 36 degree 30 minutes, with the exception of Missouri, whereas any future states south of this line would be slave states. Thus slavery was extended towards the west, with the same north/south divide.

The issue came to the fore once more in 1849 when California petitioned to join the Union. It acceded as a free state but in order to mollify the slave states, Congress agreed that while California would be free, the people of the New Mexico and Utah territories would decide whether they would be slave or free states. The compromise also required that people in free states help to capture runaway slaves. This led to a considerable heightening of tension between free and slave states, as both took up opposing positions on the moral high ground – the people of free states objecting to being co-opted as slave-catchers while those in slave states considered their Northern brethren were flouting the law.

Free and slave states of America in 1857

WASHINGTON Free by Act of 1848, conditionally to slavery by Dred Scott.

OREGON TERR. Free by Act of 1848. Opened unconditionally to slavery by the Dred Scott decision, 1857.

CALIFORNIA Admitted as a Free State 1850.

NEBRASKA TERRITORY Free by the Missouri Compromise Act of 1820. Opened conditionally to slavery by Nebraska Act of 1854. Opened unconditionally to slavery by the Dred Scott decision of 1857.

KANSAS TERRITORY 1. Free by Mexican law. 2. Opened conditionally to slavery (when formed into states) by Compromise Acts of 1850. 3. Opened unconditionally to slavery by Dred Scott decision 1857.

MO. COMPROMISE LINE 1820 36°30'

FREE STATES

SLAVE STATES

CANADA

MEXICO

Slaves bringing in cotton from the fields in South Carolina in the 1860s

As America expanded west, the issue of whether the states petitioning for accession to the Union should be slave or free came up more and more frequently. Just four years after California's accession, Illinois Senator Stephen Douglas made another attempt at a solution. As slave states had no interest in allowing new free states into the Union, the westward expansion of the United States had stopped at the Mississippi River. To get it going again, he proposed a new bill, the Kansas-Nebraska Act, which decreed that popular sovereignty would decide the issue of whether these new states should be free or slave. Many of Douglas's fellow Democrats considered this a ploy to expand slavery and they began to join with other politicians into what would become the Republican Party, united by its opposition to slavery.

BLEEDING KANSAS

When delegates elected in Kansas came to decide whether the state would be free or slave, the votes were skewed by people crossing the border from Missouri to vote for Kansas becoming a slave state. Indeed, so widespread was the fraud that two votes were cast for every registered voter. Thus, the Kansas legislature passed pro-

slavery laws. But so outraged were free state-supporting Kansans at this fraud that they began to arm themselves, creating a parallel legislature, while increasingly violent confrontations broke out between free staters and slavery supporters, who called themselves the Law and Order Party. It was a nasty conflict. In revenge for a murder, free staters burned and terrorized pro-slavery settlers, before being themselves pursued and surrounded in the town of Lawrence. In the ensuing siege, abolitionist women smuggled guns hidden in their petticoats to the besieged free staters.

The siege was called off in the midst of a cold winter, but when the slavery supporters returned to Lawrence in the spring, they burned the Free State Hotel and threw the press of the abolitionist paper, *The Herald of Freedom*, into the river. Back in the East, Republican-supporting papers wrote the event up as the 'Sack of Lawrence'.

One abolitionist, a man named John Brown, on his way to help in the defense of Lawrence, heard that he was too late but, enraged by the events, led a party of men to Pottawatomie Creek where they murdered five pro-slavery settlers. After what came to be

called the Pottawatomie Massacre, Brown took up guerrilla tactics, fighting skirmishes against pro-slavery militias. Some historians consider these small battles the first of the Civil War. And with the notoriety Brown had acquired through his actions in Kansas, he was able to gather funds for his attack on Harpers Ferry in West Virginia, where he hoped to gain arms to raise a general slave revolt. The raid failed, and Brown was captured, tried and hung for treason. The attack so inflamed passions on either side that it all but made war inevitable. On the morning of his execution, Brown wrote, "I, John Brown, am now quite certain that the crimes of this guilty land will never be purged away but with blood."

Within 18 months of Brown's execution, the American Civil War began.

SLAVERY IN THE CARIBBEAN AND SOUTH AMERICA

We know the tropical paradise of the Caribbean and South America from postcards, yet the perfect fertile landscape and sandy beaches carry long, deep-rooted histories of torture, exploitation and human bondage often forgotten

Written by Helena Neimann

View of a sugar plantation in Antilles, in what was then the French West Indies. The engraving is from an 18th century encyclopedia of arts and sciences, and presents its subject as exotically rural, ignoring the horrors of slavery

For hundreds of years, bondage was the dominant human condition in the Caribbean, and South America, defined by horrific violence and exploitation of the enslaved peoples, who were likely not to survive the inhuman conditions of the plantation. They would end their lives as slaves in captivity, far away from their lives as individuals with families, memories, and dreams in their homeland. Despite the unimaginable conditions the enslaved endured for the sake of securing goods for European tastebuds, they also courageously revolted against the occupying forces and fought for their freedom.

It is estimated that more than 12 million people were captured from their local homes in Africa and forced across the Middle Passage to an unknown land to be enslaved labor resources in the sugar, cotton, coffee and tobacco fields of South America, the Caribbean and North America between the mid-15th and mid-19th centuries. The Europeans occupied these foreign lands across the Atlantic Ocean in the pursuit of wealth and power at the cost of millions of peoples' lives and their freedom.

Ever since Columbus set foot on the Caribbean island of what today is the Bahamas on his first voyage in 1492, the Caribbean region was the battleground for European powers, including Britain and France. The Caribbean islands had the ideal position for European economic exploitation with the easy accessibility of the island shores, the islands' small sizes and long coastlines, which allowed the European ships of goods and slaves to move smoothly to and from the region. By the 17th century, slavery was established as the dominant labor system across the Caribbean. Here, the enslaved Africans were forced to work in sugar, indigo,

Tools of slavery on display in Cuba

A group of liberated slaves on the parade at Fort Augusta, Jamaica

and tobacco fields, which all required extensive manual labor, with no mercy from the plantation owners. The enslaved peoples were treated as non-human: they had no legal rights, were tortured daily, were not allowed to get married, and potential children would be sold off separately, just to name a few of the violations of basic human rights they experienced.

The cultivation of the crops that suited the European buyers transformed the original landscape of the islands. It became organized fields, where the fertile land was divided into plantations owned by separate masters. Here, the

An overseer in Brazil inflicts terrible injuries on a slave as a 'punishment' for wrongdoing

Images: all Getty Images except Almay (overseer)

The Haitian Revolution began as a slave revolt and ended with the founding of an independent state

land was arranged in straight lines, so the slaves could be watched by their owners at all times. It was a structure that was capable of resisting social and political changes and remained in the Caribbean for more than 300 years. The longevity of the colonization of the islands of the Caribbean was instrumental in creating the modern world. The region was the initial site of contact between peoples formerly separated by oceans, new modes of economic organization and new forms of social relations. The prominent scholar Sidney Mintz famously proclaimed that the Caribbean was 'modern before modernity' as it was in this region that the social, political, and economic landscape that we know and live in today was established.

One of the biggest and most famous slave revolts happened in the French colony of Saint Dominigue (known as Haiti today), where an efficient and highly profitable production line of sugar, indigo, and coffee, dependent on the unfree labor of enslaved peoples, had been constructed. At the time of the revolution, it was the wealthiest colony under the French Empire, producing 40 percent of the sugar and 60 percent of the coffee imported to European markets that were hungry for both delights. As with other colonies in the Caribbean, the largest proportion

of the population were enslaved Africans, as the sugar plantations covered much of the fertile land and the hostile tropical disease environment made sure that there was never copious White settlement on the islands. Inspired by European and African ideas of justice and freedom, the slave and vodou houngan (priest) Dutty Boukman led the first slave rebellion on the island in 1791, which grew to include thousands of participants and destroyed hundreds of plantations. In 1804, the Haitian Revolution succeeded and Haiti declared its sovereignty after defeating Napoleon Bonaparte's forces after 12 years of conflict. One of the famous leaders in the revolution was the hero Toussaint L'Ouverture, whose incredible political mastery and power grabs helped to secure the emergence of the Haitian nation. It became the first independent nation in the Caribbean and Latin America, and the only state in history created after a successful slave revolt. The legacy of the Haitian Revolution cannot be overstated: it remains a constant reminder of the perseverance, courage, and power of the enslaved who rose up against an oppressing brutal system and regained their and their nation's freedom. Yet despite the great example Haiti created as the first free Black republic to other colonies, slavery persisted in various places, most significantly in

> ## *"The Haitian Revolution remains a constant reminder of the perseverance, courage, and power of the enslaved"*

The Jamaican Maroons

The Caribbean island of Jamaica became the largest colony in the British Empire. The island witnessed frequent revolt by the maroons, a name for runaway slaves derived from the Spanish word 'cimarron', which means 'fierce' or 'unruly'. The former enslaved peoples ran away from their Spanish-owned plantations when the British took over control of the island in 1655. They escaped to the mountains and created independent communities as free peoples with their own culture, traditions, and military. In 1728, the First Maroon War between the Jamaican government and the maroons began. With community maroon leaders such as Cudjoe and Queen Nanny, the maroons successfully fought back against the British military forces, with the guerrilla warfare ending in a peace agreement that would allow the maroons to maintain their self-governed community in 1734.

Queen Nanny is an icon in Jamaica today, celebrated as the leader of the maroon settlement Nanny Town, located in the region of the Blue

A $500 Jamaican banknote from 1994, showing the iconic heroine Nanny of the Maroons

Mountains in Jamaica, and known as a great warrior, strategist and obeah woman, who prepared the maroon troupes for the attacks from their British enemies. The village led by Queen Nanny still exists and is known as Moore Town or New Nanny Town. Queen Nanny features in a range of songs and poems as well as on the $500 bill, also in slang known as a nanny, reflecting the powerful legacy and sign of hopefulness and strength that the maroons still inspire across the Caribbean today.

An overseer watches over enslaved workers during a meal following the coffee harvest on a Brazilian plantation

Slaves harvest sugar cane on a plantation, watched by a whip-wielding overseer

A view of a Jamaican sugar plantation, produced for a French audience, that glosses over the atrocities slaves experienced

Brazil, where it did not end until 1888.

While France and Britain concentrated on the Caribbean, Spain and Portugal colonized parts of Central and South America, with most of the area south of Mexico owned by one of the two nations. The relatively close position of South America, particularly Brazil, to the west coast of Africa, made it significantly cheaper and easier to move the slaves across the Atlantic Ocean than to North America. It was therefore not in the economic interest of the plantation owners to keep the enslaved for multiple generations, as they constantly had easy access to fresh cheap labor for their plantations. Compared with the North American system of enslavement, the death rate of the enslaved in Caribbean, Dutch Guiana, and Brazil was significantly higher and the birth rate much lower, so the Europeans could not sustain the population of enslaved labor without continuing the large import of Africans to the colonies. For that reason, the slaves in North America were often more generations removed from their African heritage than those in the Caribbean and South America. Looking at the statistics, they support this: of around 12 million Africans taken from their homeland, only about 450,000 of these arrived in the United States whereas 4.8 million Africans went to Brazil alone. Indeed Brazil, as a Portuguese colony and then as an independent state, was the most constant and numerous importer of enslaved Africans over the centuries. About 43 percent of all slaves brought to the Americas ended up in Brazil. Over

97 million Brazilians in a total population of 190 million people today have a significant amount of African genetic ancestry, self-identifying as either Brown (parda) or Black (preta) in the federal census (among five categories, including White [branca], Yellow [amarela], and Indigenous, Brown, and Black). Like the Caribbean colonies, Brazil needed the enslaved to sustain its major production of goods. The records show that coffee had a staggering growth: the 125,000 tons exported between 1821 and 1825 had rocketed to 1.5 million tons from 1851 to 1855. This happened because of two related reasons: the huge numbers of imported African slaves to undertake the labor-intensive work, and the explosive increase in coffee consumption, especially in the United States. By the mid-19th century, Brazil's slaves were producing half the world's coffee and by 1900, Brazil produced five times as much coffee as the rest of the world put together. Brazil is still the largest producer of coffee in the world today. It is a billion-dollar industry, which still to this day is characterized by the slave-like conditions for many of its workers that clearly continues to violate human rights.

The histories of slavery in the Caribbean and South America are often overlooked, but both places were destinations for the millions of enslaved Africans who survived the Middle Passage and stepped onto the foreign shores to meet, survive, and protest the hell of the slave societies that they found themselves a part of.

BRITAIN'S DARK PAST

Britain, the country that ended the slave trade, profited from it hugely too

Written by Edoardo Albert

In the early Medieval period, the British Isles were notorious for slavery, even after the institution had been all but extinguished in the rest of Europe following its conversion to Christianity. But the Anglo-Saxons and Celtic peoples continued to trade prisoners of war into slavery until the Norman Conquest. While no one could call William I a gentle soul, he stamped out slavery in his new kingdom and it remained largely unknown until the sudden, huge expansion of European horizons in the late 15th and 16th centuries. Sailing ships that to us would look barely robust enough to cross a lake crossed oceans, sailing south down and around Africa, and west, to the Americas.

It was a heady, exciting, and turbulent time, with fortunes to be made over those blue horizons. Among the men who set off in search of fortune was one John Lok, who set off for Africa in 1554 in a flotilla of three ships. Reaching Guinea, Lok and his sailors traded goods along the coast before turning for home in February 1555. 24 seamen died during the voyage but the expedition was considered a huge success on account of the vast wealth that Lok brought back, including 400 pounds of gold, 250 elephant tusks, and 36 butts of pepper (a hugely valuable commodity). Alongside the gold and ivory, Lok also brought back five Africans, whom he intended to learn English so that they could act as interpreters on future trading voyages. The status of these Africans is not clear from the historical record, and nor is that of the Africans that Plymouth merchant William Towerson brought back in 1557 after a similarly successful trading voyage – they may have been intended more as wonders and curiosities rather than slaves.

The Portuguese had been the first to open the route south around the tip of Africa and into the Indian Ocean. The wealth that flowed from these new trade links to the Indies and the new Portuguese territories in South America transformed the country from an impoverished backwater on the westernmost fringes of Europe to the world's first truly global empire. To protect the lucrative African trade, the Portuguese set up forts along the coast, heavily fortified emplacements at which their ships called to do business with the kings of the African interior. While the Portuguese were first, rival European maritime powers soon followed, establishing their own forts along the coast.

The trade with the interior depended absolutely on the cooperation of local African rulers since the endemic malaria of the interior led to a local European life expectancy of less than a year. Extensive, and lucrative all round, trade relationships were established, with the European merchants arriving at their forts in ships laden with high-value, luxury items that they then traded for even more valuable African ivory, spices and, increasingly, people. For across the Atlantic, in America and on the Caribbean islands, new crops were being planted that were both valuable and extremely labor intensive: tobacco, cotton, and sugar.

At first, planters tried to exploit Native Americans to tend and harvest their crops, but European diseases ravaged the indigenous Americans and familiarity with local areas allowed them to escape relatively easily back to their own peoples. Important and influential religious voices were raised against the exploitation of South American Indians. The planters then tried importing labor from Europe in the form of transported convicts and indentured laborers, poor people whose passage across the Atlantic was paid in return for a period, usually seven years, of work for their sponsor. Neither avenue provided enough hands for the labor, particularly on the Caribbean islands where yellow fever was a particular scourge.

So the Portuguese and the Spanish started importing African slaves to their American colonies. Black Africans, having been transported

by William Jackson

Sancho: A freed slave

Ignatius Sancho was a former slave who became a British writer, composer, and campaigner against the slave trade. Sancho was born in the noxious conditions of the Middle Passage as his mother was transported across the Atlantic in 1729; she died at some point not long after the slave ship arrived in South America. Only two, Sancho was taken to England by his owner and given to three sisters living in Greenwich. Sancho lived with the sisters from 1731 to 1749, there becoming known to John, Duke of Montagu. The duke was a philanthropist, one of the backers of the Foundling Hospital in London, and he quickly noted the intelligence displayed by Sancho, giving the boy books from his library to help him learn to read.

About 20 years old, well read, and intelligent, Sancho could bear slavery no longer and he ran away, finding a welcome in the duke's London home, Montagu House. There, he became butler to the duchess while furthering his education. The duchess died in 1751 but she left Sancho an annuity of £30 (£7,000 today) and Sancho married Anne Osborne in 1758. The couple had seven children and remained devoted to each other.

Sancho became a correspondent and friend to many eminent figures. In particular, his correspondence with novelist Laurence Sterne became an important foundation of the growing abolitionist movement. "It is by the finest tints, and most insensible gradations, that nature descends from the fairest face about St James's, to the sootiest complexion in Africa: at which tint of these, is it, that the ties of blood are to cease? And how many shades must we descend lower still in the scale, 'ere mercy is to vanish with them? – but 'tis no uncommon thing, my good Sancho, for one half of the world to use the other half of it like brutes, & then endeavour to make 'em so."

Portrait of an African, **attributed to Allan Ramsay, and now believed to depict a young Ignatius Sancho**

across the ocean to a strange new world, were far more dislocated than enslaved Native Americans, making it much harder for them to abscond. They also proved somewhat less prone to the diseases that cut a swathe through imported European labor. And once the slave ships had unloaded their human cargo, they filled their holds with sugar, cotton and tobacco for the return trip to Europe. The triangular Atlantic slave trade was slowly being established.

The British, as shown by John Lok and William Towerson, were not initially involved in the slave trade. But that began to change in 1562 when John Hawkins was commissioned as a privateer by Queen Elizabeth I. A group of aristocratic Tudor nobles invested in Hawkins, providing the funds for three ships to sail to Africa, where he captured 300 slaves from the Portuguese before sailing to Santo Domingo (present-day Dominican Republic), where he sold the slaves in exchange for sugar, pearls, and hides. The trip proved so fabulously lucrative that Elizabeth allowed Hawkins a coat of arms that showed a slave with lion passant and bezants. There was money in trading slaves but it was not until the restoration of the Stuart monarchy in the 17th century that the British started slave trading to any great extent.

The slave trade was driven by sugar. There was an insatiable demand for sugar and, in the 1640s, Dutch traders brought sugar cane to Barbados. The Dutch had appropriated the knowledge of how to grow sugar cane from Brazilian plantations that they had captured

The Westerly Side of the Castle at Mina

Elmina Castle, the first Portuguese trading post built on the Gulf of Guinea. Heavily fortified, it became the model for the slave trading posts dotted around the coast of Africa

Planting sugar cane in the West Indies

and, in Barbados, they found famers eager to learn how to grow the new crop. Barbados was a British possession and in its early years the farmers there had established small farms growing a mixture of crops, cotton, and tobacco. But sugar changed everything. Big landowners bought out or muscled out the smaller farmers and established huge plantations growing fields of sugar cane.

Growing sugar cane is labor intensive and, at first, Barbadian planters tried to fill their fields with transported convicts and indentured laborers. But the Dutch had also introduced African slaves with the sugar cane and, what was more, they seemed able to provide a stream of new slaves to replace those who died – and the attrition rate was high, with the slaves being worked hard and punished harder. With greed driving growth, the Barbadian elite bought in more and more slaves while passing laws that fixed their status as property rather than human beings. The slave trade was moving into its industrial phase.

"The company's directors quickly realized there was more money in trading people than trading gold"

As the trade in sugar exploded, it was the Dutch who provided the British-owned plantations in the Caribbean with slaves. But by a series of laws known as the Navigation Acts, the British government sought to squeeze the Dutch out of this trade and replace them with British ships and merchants. One of the first steps towards this was the establishment of the Company of Royal Adventurers Trading into Africa in 1660. Among its investors was Charles II and his brother, the Duke of York, later James II, as well as City of London merchants. Originally intended to trade gold, the Company was granted the monopoly in trading slaves in 1663 and the company's directors quickly

realized there was more money in trading people than trading gold.

Having been granted a monopoly in trade from Africa, the company, renamed the Royal African Company in 1672, policed the coastal waters, seizing rivals (known as 'interlopers'). The goods and ships seized were sold with the Company receiving half the proceeds and the Crown the other half. The forts, known as factories, along the coast from which the Company conducted its business were heavily fortified, with stockades, known as barracoons, where the African captives awaiting transportation into slavery were held in captivity awaiting the arrival of the slave ships.

47

A model showing a cross-section through a typical slave ship during the Middle Passage

By the 1680s, the Royal African Company was shipping 5,000 people a year across the Atlantic. It was the single largest shipper of slaves across the ocean and many of those slaves were branded with the letters 'DoY', standing for the Duke of York: James, brother of King Charles II, the Company's governor and, from 1685 until 1688, king of England and Scotland. When James was deposed in the Glorious Revolution of 1688, the incoming government of William and Mary revoked the Royal African Company's monopoly on trade with Africa as many of their supporters were eager to get a slice of the highly lucrative slave trade.

In 1698, the slave trade was opened up to any merchant who could raise the finance to fund a voyage and, in the accompanying scramble, the slave trade exploded. Historians estimate that up to 1807, when the slave trade was declared illegal in Britain, British ships and merchants transported 3.1 million African men, women, and children to the Americas and Caribbean, almost half a million of whom didn't survive the voyage.

The Atlantic slave trade turned small British ports into rich cities, while also further enriching London. Between 1700 and 1800, Britain's economy pivoted dramatically, turning away from Europe and towards the Atlantic. Britain sent 82 percent of its exports to Europe in 1700. A century later, only 21 percent of the country's exports went across the Channel; 61 percent went into the Atlantic economy. What's more, exports quadrupled during the century. They sailed from Bristol, Liverpool, and Glasgow, turning them into rich and important cities.

The explosion in Atlantic trade was not by any means solely driven by slaves. The exact proportion of the British economy derived from slavery remains controversial, with historians and economists offering widely differing estimates. Some claim that slavery financed the Industrial Revolution, while others say it contributed only a tiny fraction of the investment that changed Britain from a rural to an urban economy.

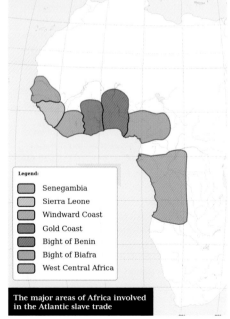

Legend:
- Senegambia
- Sierra Leone
- Windward Coast
- Gold Coast
- Bight of Benin
- Bight of Biafra
- West Central Africa

The major areas of Africa involved in the Atlantic slave trade

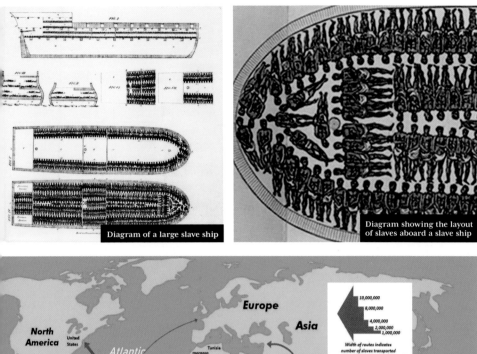

Diagram of a large slave ship

Diagram showing the layout of slaves aboard a slave ship

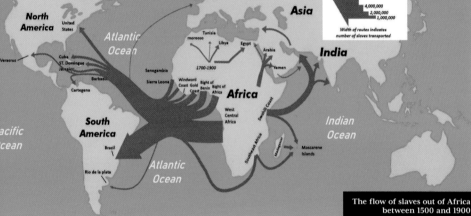

The flow of slaves out of Africa between 1500 and 1900

merchant class. Many of the merchants involved in the slave trade endowed their home cities with foundations and charitable works. Edward Colston, whose statue was toppled into Bristol dock in 2020, gave his home city £100,000 (roughly £21 million today) to fund charitable endeavors, including a school and almshouses.

For the British, the slave trade largely continued out of sight; there were very few domestic slaves in Britain, with the law remaining unsettled as to whether anyone could be a slave in Britain. However, in 1772, in the case of Somerset vs Stewart, Lord Mansfield ruled that James Somerset, an African slave brought to England by his owner, Charles Stewart, could not be removed from Britain against his will. The case drew wide attention, becoming a focus for the burgeoning abolitionist movement, and while legal scholars continue to discuss the exact ramifications of Lord Mansfield's judgement, the British public quickly came to take it as meaning that, on English soil, no man could be a slave.

Over the next 35 years, the campaign against the slave trade grew in Britain, despite the opposition of entrenched and wealthy interests, and in 1807 Parliament passed the Act for the Abolition of the Slave Trade. Britain, and its navy, then turned its attention to stamping out a trade that it had done so much to facilitate earlier. That was not the end, however: the Slavery Abolition Act was passed in 1833, entering law in 1834. Slavery was fully abolished in the territories of the British Empire in 1838. In 1102, the Council of London had ruled, "Let no one dare hereafter to engage in the infamous business, prevalent in England, of selling men like animals." Many millions had suffered to return to the law of the Middle Ages.

"For the British, the slave trade largely continued out of sight"

In its most developed form, the trade took manufactured goods, particularly guns and weapons, cloth, iron, and beer from Britain to Africa. There, merchants exchanged these goods for slaves, as well as ivory, gold, and spices, and shipped them across the Atlantic on the notorious Middle Passage to the Caribbean and North America. There, the slaves were sold and exchanged for sugar, molasses, and wood in the Caribbean, and rice, silk, indigo, and tobacco in North America, which were then transported back across the Atlantic to Britain. There were profits to be made at each stage of the trade, making a successful voyage highly lucrative. However, both the general perils of the sea and

the particular dangers of the diseases endemic in Africa and the Caribbean meant that a high number of sailors died alongside the high number of slave casualties.

The raw materials brought from the Caribbean and North America, particularly cotton, were important drivers of the Industrial Revolution. Cotton factories, driven by new steam and water technologies, multiplied the amount of cotton that could be processed hugely. By 1800, a cotton spinner could spin 200 times more cotton than his predecessor a century earlier. Wool had been the basis of England's wealth in the Middle Ages, but in the 18th and 19th centuries cotton became Britain's biggest export.

This explosion in trade was reflected in the growth of the three major Atlantic ports: Bristol, Liverpool, and Glasgow. Between 1700 and 1800, they grew hugely, with Glasgow's population quadrupling. As trade expanded, all the ancillary industries involved in shipping grew to supply the demands of Britain's increasingly wealthy

The coat of arms awarded to Sir John Hawkins following his lucrative voyage: note the slave at the top

THE HUMAN EXPERIENCE

Uncover the horrific realities of slavery for millions of men, women, and children

The Slave Ship by JMW Turner was produced in 1840, but is widely considered to have been inspired by the story of the Zong massacre, depicting African people being thrown to sharks in the Atlantic Ocean

A JOURNEY IN CHAINS

*A waterway of murder, disease, torture, and death,
the Middle Passsage is the greatest unmarked graveyard in history*

Written by Arisa Loomba

The Middle Passage denotes the journey across the stretch of Atlantic Ocean waterways taken by innumerable ships carrying enslaved people from the African coast to destinations throughout the Americas. At least 12 million people were transported across the Middle Passage over a period of 400 years: the largest single forced migration of people in history, and a highly traumatic one that lives on today in the collective memories of Black communities across the world.

It was during the Middle Passage that free people were made into slaves. It was part of a process of the commodification of human beings. These people were 'manufactured' into slaves through three key phases: warehousing (held captive on the African coast in forts, prisons, and barracoons, waiting to be loaded onto ships); transport (tightly packed and shipped across the ocean); packaging and delivery (as the captives neared the Americas, they were cleaned up and forced to exercise, before being disembarked, marketed, and sold to new owners).

In Africa, local ruling groups and merchants were vital intermediaries supporting the running of the system. The captive Africans' experience of hunger, thirst, abuse, and exhaustion began long before the official commencement of

Slavers kidnapping Africans and sending them on slave ships

the Middle Passage journey. Really, the Middle Passage began in the interior of the African continent, from which men, women, and children were chained together in coffles, and escorted by merchants on a long enforced march to the sea. Imprisoned in dark underground dungeons and pens, the sense of disorientation, terror, and confusion that unravelled and dismantled people's spirits and sense of self, was only just beginning.

FROM HUMAN TO POSSESSION

The Royal African Company employed extensive networks of agents across both African and American ports to receive and scrutinize captives. At the coast, White ship captains assessed the physical potential of the enslaved before agreeing to load them aboard: what value they might bring to a plantation owner. It was not just men who were assessed. Women represented indispensable sexual assets, and were selected according to notions of aesthetic beauty. Indeed, beauty standards may have possessed an underestimated force in the slave

market. They were shackled to other captives to prevent escape or freedom of movement. Some people would jump into the water and commit suicide before this happened, so that they might never have to leave their homeland.

The journey from Africa to the Americas was long, arduous, and treacherous. In the early days, it could take on average 133 days to cross the Atlantic. As shipping design and technology changed over the centuries, the journey became much quicker, and by 1820, it only took around

50 days. Before disembarking, slaves' grey hair was dyed black and beards shaved to make them look younger. Sores were covered, skin rubbed in palm oil, and the rectums of dysentery sufferers plugged with rope to prevent indiscreet leakage. All of this was to ensure the captives were at

their optimum marketability.

The building of infrastructure to furnish the Middle Passage was immense, and employed laborers and skilled workers across so many industries and regions. Even just the building of the ships drew innumerable sectors into the slave trade. Glaziers, ship builders, oar makers, masons, ropers, canvas makers, iron and tin workers, woodworkers, upholsterers, and many more innocent and innocuous laborers played their part to make the trade possible. The

"Women represented indispensable sexual assets, and were selected according to notions of aesthetic beauty"

ships were fitted with swivel guns that could be pointed at the slaves on deck at all times. An extensive set of torture instruments was also within easy reach: gags, masks, muskets, ropes, whips, shackles, neck rings, force-feeding devices, branding irons, and collars were just

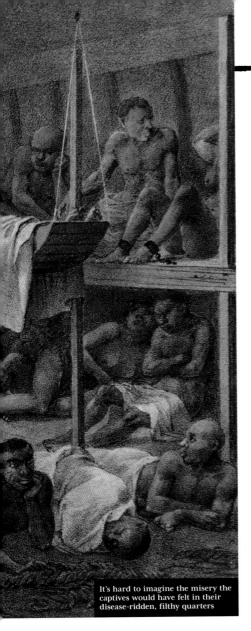

It's hard to imagine the misery the captives would have felt in their disease-ridden, filthy quarters

some of these. Professional musicians and surgeons lived aboard the ships, and people were promoted or rotated across many different roles. The slave trade was abolished in the British Empire in 1807, which should have seen the last of the slave vessels crossing the Middle Passage. Yet, an illegal trade continued to ship several thousand human beings to the United States and other parts of the Americas until well into the 19th century. The last ship to arrive in the US

Captives being brought on board a slave ship on the west coast of Africa, c1880

The Zong massacre: bringing the Middle Passage home

In 1781, a curious, horrifying incident took place aboard a slave ship called the Zong, that got the world talking. For the first time, it prompted a major questioning of the practice of slavery in Britain. All of a sudden, the slave trade did not feel like something that happened far away in exotic lands. Everyone was implicated in some way, and Britain bore a responsibility for what took place on the Middle Passage.

In this year, a Liverpool slaving company run by William Gregson sent out a slave ship to the Cape Coast of Africa, called the William. It took several months to fill up the ship with captured people. In the meantime, the British government had seized a Dutch ship, the Zorg, which contained 244 Africans already, and put it up for sale, captives and all. Gregson bought it, and forced 196 more slaves into the hold. This was far too many for the size of the ship, but more slaves equalled more profit, so overcrowding was common. They decided to change the ship's name to the Zong and cobbled together a woefully small crew from the William.

Four months later, the Zong set sail, bound for Black River, Jamaica. It then transpired that the ship had overshot its destination, and the journey was taking much longer than it should. Though the crew believed they had enough water, they had missed a stop to replenish their supplies. The inexperienced crew had not accounted for what would happen in this event. There simply was not enough water for the whole ship to survive on. The captain, Luke Collingwood, ordered the Africans to be killed in three batches. This would slowly reduce the burden on the water, in the hopes that the fittest, most marketable slaves could be saved and hopefully make it alive. By this point, some of the captives had already been imprisoned on the ship for a year. The weakest and most vulnerable had no choice or chance. One hundred and thirty two human beings were thrown overboard to meet their fate.

Initially, the only reason that this case was brought to public attention – for it was certainly not the first of its kind – was because the Gregson Syndicate sued their insurers for compensation for the loss of 132 cargo. There was no immediate outrage. There was no cover up.

Gregson knew that there was nothing to hide, there was no chance of the case being challenged as murder. The thought would not have even crossed their minds. Indeed, they were readily given the insurance money they demanded. It was only later that Olaudah Equiano, a freed slave living in London, read of the case in the newspaper. He brought it to the experienced abolitionist Granville Sharp, and together, they fought to appeal the case in 1783 on the grounds of murder. They were the first people to suggest that the African slaves were, in fact, human beings, and that their deaths were wilful murders. The appeal was quickly shot down and ultimately failed. However, the impacts of what Equiano and Sharp did go much beyond the legal result. For one of the first times, the question finally arose; was this murder? Were they humans or were they cargo? Would it have ever have even crossed anyone's minds to throw White people overboard in the event of a water shortage? What does it mean to be a human being?

The story of the Zong massacre should not be shocking, or seen as an isolated case. It was no different to many other massacres that took place in similar circumstances. Conveniently, very few primary sources exist on the Zong massacre, much less any indication for what the experience may have been like for the Africans aboard the ship. But the national conversation, and surge in support for the abolition movement that it produced, was certainly unprecedented, as was the illumination of the legal and moral questions of slavery and the crimes of the Middle Passage. It became clear that in order to change the slave trade, legal change was required. This became the focus of the abolition movement henceforth.

Contemporary woodcut of slaves being thrown overboard during the Zong massacre in 1781

was the Clotilda in 1860.

Yet, only about five percent of Middle Passage ships went to the USA. Ten times as many went to Brazil and the Caribbean islands respectively. The main population aboard the ships was male. But women and children were in high demand too, particularly in the early days of the slave trade: up to 45 percent of slave ship captives could be women. Interestingly, the proportion of children (mainly young boys) only rose over time from five or ten percent in the 17th century, to 50 percent in the 19th century. Nearly half of all enslaved Africans came from the regions of Angola and the Kingdom of Kongo. After this, the next most important region was the Bight of Benin, along Africa's 'Slave Coast', followed by the Bight of Biafra. Planters in the Americas frequently expressed preferences and requests for slaves from particular ethnic groups who exhibited 'favorable' skills, knowledge, characteristics, or behaviors. For instance, people from the Gold Coast were known to have extensive experience in rice cultivation. This knowledge was desired on the rice paddies of South Carolina. On the other hand, Igbo people were thought to be meek, docile, loyal, and obedient. Thus, they were trusted and favored as domestic servants living in the big houses.

"The smell and toxicity would have lingered despite cleaning"

Disease began to spread in the pens along the coast, weakening morale and strength to resist even before the journey began. Enslaved people were transferred between different ships to fill them up as quickly as possible, intensifying the transfer of bacteria and illness across the population. The tight packing of men and women in airless spaces only hastened the spread.

Another horrifying cause of disease was a result of having bodily fluids and excrement moving freely around the hold, causing skin diseases, foul smells, and the rampant spread of toxic bacteria. These fluids sunk into the wooden structures of the ship, and could not be easily scrubbed away. The smell and toxicity would have lingered despite cleaning, which was sometimes done while captives were made to exercise on the deck. The air in the hold would have been stagnant, and breathing would have become laborious. Their bodies became slowly accustomed to the air quality, and when forced onto the deck, many would faint or even die due to the shock of pure air hitting their lungs.

Captives could not clean themselves, apart from an occasional opportunity to use a shared

Insurrection Aboard a Slave Ship, **1851 lithograph. The crew fires at a slave revolt with many slaves jumping overboard**

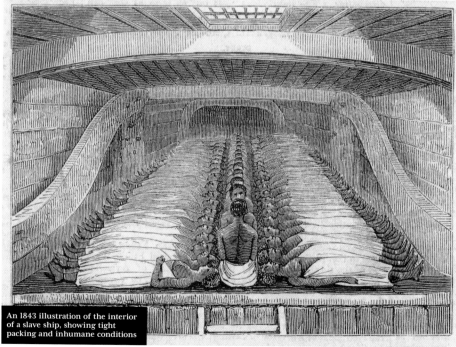

An 1843 illustration of the interior of a slave ship, showing tight packing and inhumane conditions

The famous Brookes slave ship. A 1787 engraving depicting the ideal method of packing slaves onto a ship. This image became one of the most powerful symbols of the abolitionist cause

African captives fight against an 18th century slave ship crew. Captives greatly outnumbered the ships' crew

basin of water. Washing communally, however, hardly provided the prospect of actually getting clean. In the stagnant water, bodily fluids sloshed around, transferring between bodies and being ingested when faces were washed. The stagnant water tubs attracted flies and vermin, which also harbored diseases. The only grooming offered was the forcible shaving of head and body hair, which was removed to keep away lice and parasites, and prevent it from being matted in excrement and fluids. Nonetheless, washing, and sometimes being given the chance to rub palm oil over their bodies afterwards to prevent skin diseases and dryness, offered slaves the illusion of bodily care and control, self-possession, and dignity.

UNCHECKED CONDITIONS

There were debates regarding the relative merit of tightly packing as many slaves as possible onto a ship and risking many deaths from illness, or boarding fewer slaves in safer, more spacious conditions. A conclusion was never reached, and thus the fate of many people was dictated by the type, size and density of people aboard

the ship they were forced onto. Captains usually purchased more people than they needed, well aware of the likelihood of mass death along the way. Slave ships gained a nasty reputation and stigma for the smell they produced. And yet, there were no regulations placed on the way slave vessels should be constructed. It was mostly down to individual discretion and needs. As time went on, though, the general design and standard of slave vessels did change to increase airflow and make cleaning and sterilization easier, as it became clear that there were ways to prevent loss of life, or cargo, as they saw it. Ship death rates did decline over time, from 26 percent in the early 17th century, to ten percent at the height of the trade in the late 18th and early 19th centuries. However, the final year or two of the slave trade, before its full abolition in 1808, saw a surge in deaths as captains scrambled to get as many people out of Africa as possible, while it was still legal.

Food for the journey came from different parts of the Atlantic and was cobbled together. In England, captains loaded beans, flour, bread, oats, biscuits, butter, liquor, and meat. While

docked in Africa they picked up plantains and bananas, palm oil, dried fish, cassava, rice and other grains, brandy, and most importantly, yams. There was a huge reliance on yams on slave voyages, as they kept well on the long journeys and did not go bad. Fresh fruits or vegetables were rare due to high temperatures and unpredictable weather patterns leaving them susceptible to rot. It was common for rats and pests, such as weevils and maggots, to destroy food supplies, or for them to become damp, moldy and inedible. Ensuring the ship had enough water at all times was also a challenge that required planning and skill. To save water, the slaves could instead be given brandy and rum, which only served to increase their delirium and disorientation.

ENHANCED ISOLATION

The people aboard the ship would have originated from many different cultural, linguistic, ethnic, and religious groups. The sense of terror was added to by the fact that people could often not find others with whom they spoke a shared language. The isolation and confusion was immense. Slavers would capitalize on this, purposely shackling together two men who spoke different languages, to prevent them from being able to communicate and conspire to escape or revolt. Shackling men together also was intended to discourage suicide. In some cases, two men shackled together could not even

Images: Alamy

'The abolition of the slave trade or the inhumanity of dealers in human flesh exemplified in Captn Kimber's treatment of a young Negro girl of 15 for her virjen (sic) modesty'. Print shows sailor on a slave ship suspending an African girl by her ankle

An 1839 newspaper report of one of the most famous slave ship rebellions, aboard the Amistad, which took place near Cuba, and was a major trigger for the American abolitionist movement

Death of Capt. Ferrer, the Captain of the Amistad, July, 1839.

Don Jose Ruiz and Don Pedro Montez, of the Island of Cuba, having purchased fifty-three slaves at Havana, recently imported from Africa, put them on board the Amistad, Capt. Ferrer, in order to transport them to Principe, another port on the Island of Cuba. After being out from Havana about four days, the African captives on board, in order to obtain their freedom, and return to Africa, armed themselves with cane knives, and rose upon the Captain and crew of the vessel. Capt. Ferrer and the cook of the vessel were killed; two of the crew escaped; Ruiz and Montez were made prisoners.

accomplish basic tasks, so large was the language gap.

In a poor attempt to raise spirits and keep the slaves' muscles from disintegrating due to lack of movement, aid blood circulation and digestion and get some Vitamin D, the captives were forced to regularly climb up to the deck and jump up and down to the beat of a drum or the tune of a violin, in what was supposed to be 'dancing'. These dance sessions were strategically increased in frequency the closer the ship got to its destination, so that the enslaved people would arrive looking fit, healthy, and full of life. They were expected to smile and act happy and joyous during these periods: a lack of enthusiasm could result in flogging or other abuse. Though

given the language barriers and living conditions of the captives, and the crew knew this well enough. Revolts occurred on around ten percent of voyages, and it is likely that the language barrier was a key reason there wasn't more frequent insurrection. It was much easier to stage a revolt on smaller ships with fewer captives, but in all cases, it was an incredibly risky undertaking. Slaves could be killed in the battle, or be put to death or tortured as punishment if it failed. There was no exit point or opt-out if things went awry. Very few captives had the necessary sailing skills to command a ship or navigate it to free land, either. In the atmosphere of terror that was created, captives would inform on one another and reveal revolt

small-scale resistance was more common, and perhaps more threatening. Resistance came in all kinds, from dancing, singing, and sharing stories that gave people a sense of connection to their homeland and identity, despite the slavers' attempts to destroy it, to refusing to live as a slave. It was believed that in death, Africans would return to their homeland. Thus, rather than be led to an unchosen life, many decided to starve themselves to death, or launch themselves overboard when unchained on deck.

IN PLAIN SIGHT

Suicide rates were higher for women than for men. Women were unchained more often, as they were less feared than men were, and it was

"Though violent, organized resistance was extremely difficult, it certainly did happen"

humiliating, these periods were also a chance for the enslaved to stretch and breath, dance traditional steps, and connect with spirits and stories of their homelands. It was also a time for analyzing the crew and devising tactics of escape or murder.

THE THREAT OF RESISTANCE

One of the key ingredients for a victorious slave revolt, in which the slaves could successfully seize the ship by killing or imprisoning the crew, and direct it back to Africa, was collaboration and organization. This was near impossible

plans to the crew. In return, they might receive greater freedom and be unshackled, be allowed to work on the deck, receive more food and other perks. Those captives who defected into the crew by informing on fellow bond-people also experienced a much higher quality of life, perhaps being seen as closer to White, or higher class. In some rare cases though, ships did successfully arrive back in Africa after the enslaved freed themselves.

Though violent, organized resistance was extremely difficult, it certainly did happen and it made ship captains very anxious. Individual,

Crew rowing a captive to a slave ship off the coast of Africa, 1700s

not believed that they could be a threat, giving them more opportunities to jump overboard. It was not uncommon for pregnant women to abort their unborn children, or for babies to be killed by their mothers in an attempt to save them from the life that lay ahead. Other women tried to smile and laugh through whippings and torture, infuriating and tormenting the sailors who strove to break the Africans' spirits.

A famous print produced in 1792 promoting the abolitionist cause, depicts a naked Black woman strung up by her ankles upon a ship deck, while being whipped by a laughing Captain Kimber. They are observed casually by passing crew members, who appear slightly disturbed but certainly not surprised. Women were given more free rein of the ship as they were required to service the crew and were frequently sexually abused and raped. Women, with their relative freedom of movement, could collect weapons and metal, steal keys to undo shackles, gain intelligence on the whereabouts of the crew, and act as lookouts, under the guise of sex work. Statistics show that slave ship rebellions were more frequent – and more successful – on ships with higher numbers of enslaved females. The power and centrality of women to emancipation in the Middle Passage must not be overlooked. The slave ship, a floating prison, was a hotbed of dissent and rebellion of all forms, with people willing to die for their freedom. Terror prevailed for all, but experiences varied greatly according to age, gender, health and ability.

AN OCEAN OF TEARS

There was little boundary between land and sea – the continents were interlinked by these ocean spaces, keeping and hiding the many secrets of brutality that took place throughout the Atlantic world. In this way, the sea is not just a passive body of water that carried the ships. It was an active character in the story of

An engraving shows a slave revolt against slave traders in West Africa

slavery. So were the sharks that lurked in its waters, hungry participants relied on by White seamen to gobble up and destroy traces of dead bodies and shameful crimes. One 18th century publication even wrote a 'letter' written by these sharks, supposedly a humorous, comedic piece of satire, imploring the British Parliament not to abolish the slave trade, for what else would they have to eat if not the bodies of Africans? The sea was a constant zone of death, a constant zone of power struggles between Black and White, men and women, the healthy and the dying. Indeed, what makes the crimes of the Middle Passage so frightening is the fact that they took place at sea. Not only did the sea quickly swallow up and hide signs of crime, but the sea isn't owned by any one nation. It transcends all national boundaries, and so holding people, or nations accountable for the tragedies today, becomes even more difficult. How can we commemorate, remember, and mark events that took place on unnamed and unidentifiable stretches of water, over a period of 400 years?

The Middle Passage certainly didn't end at the point of disembarkation on the other side of the Atlantic. During this journey, enslaved people were slowly conditioned – through physical, sexual, emotional, and psychological abuse – into chattel. It was an initiation into the social order of violence and obedience, or captivity and confinement that would characterize much of their lives to come. Each year, more and more Africans arrived on the plantations. The new arrivals helped to keep African traditions alive across the Americas, resurrecting and reinvigorating the cultural practices of those who had been enslaved for many years. But they also kept the memory of the Middle Passage experience alive as stories were shared and passed down, becoming very much part of the story of the African diaspora.

A living hell for all aboard

Though the worst of the cruelty was undoubtedly reserved for the enslaved, there was nonetheless a hierarchy to which everyone aboard was subjected. Ordinary sailors were lower down the pecking order and were also known to stage rebellions against their mistreatment and poor working conditions. They were not exempt from receiving floggings and physical violence, even leading to death, in punishment. It seems that many sailors would escape into the Americas when the ship docked, so terrible was their experience. But perversely, this was in many ways helpful to the captain, who had no need for so many sailors to sail a ship without human cargo back to Britain. It was in the captains' interest to beat his sailors into jumping ship, so that he would not have to pay them for the journey back. Penniless, starving, homeless sailors could often be found wandering the streets of Caribbean and North American port towns, taken in by locals and even by slaves. These stories shed even more light on what a vast machine of suffering these ships operated in along the Middle Passage.

It is very difficult to understand the Middle Passage experience from the perspective of the slaves or the sailors, Black and White, as almost all, apart from the highest crew members, would have been illiterate. Most of the evidence we have of the Middle Passage comes from written sources produced by the elites of the trade. Apart from the rare surviving diaries of ordinary sailors, we find stories of these journeys within ship captains' and surgeons' accounts, records and letters. It was required to record logs of deaths in transit, sale accounts and the Middle Passage was often depicted in Parliamentary debates, accounts of legal disputes, and recollections of slave revolts. In all of this, it is possible to garner just some faint glimpses of what this experience may have been like for the diverse group of humans imprisoned on these "wooden worlds."

A sailor walks among the enslaved in the hold of the Gloria, c1850

TOOLS OF TERROR

Shackles and chains on display at the Museum Kura Hulanda in Willemstad on the Caribbean island of Curaçao. They were used to transport enslaved men, women, and children during the unimaginable horror of the Middle Passage, which could last for up to 80 days. Due to the cramped conditions, captives were shackled together lying down, side by side, head to foot, or even closer. Deaths from suffocation, malnutrition, and disease were routine.

LIFE IN CAPTIVITY

Uncover the wretched lives of the enslaved who found themselves working on the plantations of the American South

Written by Scott Reeves

Slave traders in the ports of the west Atlantic had a repulsive form of advance notice when a slave ship neared the end of the Middle Passage – a disgusting smell carried on the wind, the result of the atrocious conditions on board. Yet it was in the best interests of the ships' captains to create as good an impression as possible for prospective buyers. Traders wanted healthy, strong slaves to be sold on to the plantations of the American South. They did not want diseased or ill workers who may die or be unable to work. Nor did they want slaves who showed signs of being punished, since they might pose disciplinary problems in the future.

Slaves were removed from the ships and harshly scrubbed to remove inground dirt. Hair was combed and de-matted. Open wounds were filled with hot tar in an attempt to heal them, or at least temporarily remove the smell and puss of infection. An improved diet was offered in the few days before an auction in the hope that a slave's skin might develop a healthier luster.

Buyers were invited to examine the slaves on offer. They pulled and prodded, tested the mobility of limbs, looked at the slaves' teeth, asked questions to those who could speak English. Pulling up the skin on the top of the hand to test its elasticity was a good guide to a slave's age. Younger, healthy slaves inevitably reached the highest prices in auctions. Older, infirm, and obviously sick slaves were placed into the scramble auction. A flat price per head was agreed beforehand and buyers rushed to select the slaves they wanted.

What the buyers usually failed to consider was a slave's familial relationships. Husbands and wives were split up, parents were separated from children. One former slave recalled her mother's distressing experience: "When Ma was young, she said they put her on a block and sold her. They auctioned her off at Richmond, Virginia. When they sold her, her mother fainted or dropped dead, she never knowed which. She wanted to go and see her mother lying over there on the ground, and the man what bought her wouldn't let her. He just took her on. Drove her off like cattle, I reckon."

Even families lucky enough to be bought by the same buyer were not guaranteed to remain together. Slaves were traded within the United States regularly and a slave might expect to be bought and sold several times during their lifetime. Plantations and their owners fell into debt and were forced to sell off slaves, some sold children born to slave women as they came into working age, other slave owners simply seized any opportunity to make a profit by selling on a particular slave if the price was right.

As many as 1.2 million domestic transactions took place between 1760 and 1860, with the pace picking up after the importation of slaves into the USA was banned in 1808. Slave auctions did not just take place in ports and around the

Picking cotton was a task that took a long time and required slaves to work from sunrise to sunset

The Weeping Time

The largest single slave auction took place over two days in March 1859 near Savannah, Georgia to pay off gambling debts accrued by slave owner Pierce Mease Butler. The sale, now remembered as the Great Slave Auction or the Weeping Time, saw over 400 slaves transported by steamboat from Butler Island Plantation to Ten Broeck racecourse. The slaves were housed in horse stalls for four days before the auction began and around 200 potential buyers braved torrential rain to view them. Hidden among the traders were members of anti-slavery organizations who infiltrated the event and wrote scathing articles afterwards.

Since they had already lived and worked on a cotton plantation, many of the Butler Island slaves were skilled workers. Some were able to operate machinery, others were blacksmiths, coopers, and shoemakers. The highest price achieved for an individual slave was $1,750, the lowest was $250. By the end of the second day of the auction, 429 slaves had changed hands.

The seven unsold were ill or disabled and did not attract an offer. Family members were kept together and the catalogue insisted that they were sold together as lots. However, at least one family was separated when the buyer resold some of his purchases to new owners.

FOR SALE.
LONG COTTON AND RICE
NEGROES.

A GANG OF **460** NEGROES, accustomed to the culture of Rice and Provisions; among whom are a number of good mechanics, and house servants. Will be sold on the 2d and 3d of March next, at Savannah, by
JOSEPH BRYAN.

TERMS OF SALE.—One-third cash; remainder by bond, bearing interest from day of sale, payable in two equal annual instalments, to be secured by mortgage on the negroes, and approved personal security, or for approved city acceptance on Savannah or Charleston. Purchasers paying for papers.

The Great Slave Auction of 1859 raised $303,850, the equivalent of $10 million today

Families were often split up at slave auctions by buyers who had more interest in a slave's health, skills, and ability to work

plantations of the South. Auctions are known to have taken place at the Meal Market on Wall Street in New York between 1711 and 1762.

One of the busiest auction houses was Franklin and Armfield in Alexandria, Virginia. Its owners made a fortune taking slaves from Virginia, Maryland, and Delaware, where there was a surplus of labor in the first half of the 19th century, to the plantations of the Deep South, where there was a constant need for new workers. In 1850, nearly nine out of ten slaves in the USA lived and worked on farms or plantations dedicated to cotton, rice, sugar, and tobacco.

A MISERABLE EXISTENCE

Whether newly arrived or old hands, most plantation slaves were housed in notched-log cabins varying in size from one-room habitations to dormitory-style accommodation. They were bleak. Size was kept to a minimum, even when space was not limited on large plantations. The floor was compacted dirt. Holes and cracks between logs and planks were plugged with mud. Wooden chimneys were often ineffective, filling the cabin with smoke.

Cabins were usually not partitioned into rooms, even in those shared by multiple families. Slaves often rigged up their own dividers out of wood or cloth to maintain a scrap of privacy. It was in these crude huts that slaves had to cook, eat, and sleep. Some were locked in at night, a dark corner serving as the toilet.

Few slaves had a bed. Most slept on wooden boards or blankets on the floor, although former slave turned anti-slavery campaigner Frederick Douglass claimed, "They find less

difficulty from the want of beds, than from the want of time to sleep."

Plantation slaves were roused from their beds early by the sound of a horn and were expected to be at work within 30 minutes, sometimes before sunrise. A day of hard graft lay before them. The primary function of plantation slaves was to sow, tend, harvest, and process the crops grown in the fields.

On cotton, sugar, and tobacco plantations, where the plants needed constant care, workers were divided into gangs separated by physical ability. The most capable men and women worked in the first gang, typically joining in their late teens once they were strong enough. The manual labor was tough. After ten or 12 years, when the constant grind of physical labor took its toll, workers were relegated to the

The slave pens at Franklin and Armfield Company in Virginia featured high walls and prison-like bars on doors and windows

> *"Plantations housing more than 100 slaves developed. Discipline could be spectacularly cruel to ensure that such large numbers of slaves remained under control"*

Dancing and singing were two of the few ways that slaves kept their ancestral traditions and culture alive

By the time a slave reached around 40 years old they joined the third gang. Though their bodies were weary and worn out, they still had jobs to do. Weeding the fields was an endless battle, while the third gang was also responsible for trapping the rats that feasted on the growing sugar cane.

OTHER WORKING CONDITIONS

Work was equally difficult on other plantations. Cotton plantations were labor intensive, with field slaves picking and bundling cotton from morning to night. As cotton became the primary industry of the South, especially after the invention of the cotton gin in 1793, massive plantations housing more than 100 slaves developed. Discipline could be spectacularly cruel to ensure that such large numbers of slaves remained under control.

Tobacco plantations were more common around Virginia, Kentucky, and the Carolinas. Tobacco seeds had to be carefully tended. They were grown in frames before being transplanted into fields once the weather was warm enough. The plants were meticulously checked every day to remove flowers, forcing as much of the plant's energy as possible into the leaves, and pulling up weeds that stole vital nutrients from the soil.

The leaves were harvested as they ripened, or entire tobacco plants were dug up and hung in barns to dry and cure. Processing and packing

second gang, which carried out slightly less demanding tasks.

On sugar plantations, the soil was turned over with hoes before sugar cane was planted in late summer. The first gang dug squares around 20 centimeters deep and one meter wide, banking up the soil on each side. The second gang followed, planting two sugar cane cuttings in each hole before backfilling with soil and manure. It was back-breaking work. Each slave might be expected to dig 100 squares each day, shifting as much as 40 cubic meters (1,413 cubic foot) of soil, all carried out during the hottest days of the year. Every basket of manure, weighing around 66 pounds, had to be hauled into the field by hand. It held enough for two squares.

Slave owners hoped that slaves who created family units would be less likely to run away, although marriages between slaves were unofficial

Images: Alamy (family units), Getty Images (auction)

The planting and harvesting of sugar cane was
tough work carried out by gangs of slaves

was just as tedious as fieldwork. As Henry Clay Bruce remembered, "I was kept busy every minute from sunrise to sunset, without being allowed to speak a word to anyone. . . It was so prison-like to be compelled to sit during the entire year under a large bench or table filled with tobacco, and tie lugs all day long except during the 30 minutes allowed for breakfast and the same time allowed for dinner."

"Few slaves were overweight, many suffered from scurvy as a result of poor diet"

Rice plants were hardier and did not require the same constant level of care. As a result, slaves on rice plantations in the Carolinas tended to work under the task system rather than the gang system. Each slave was assigned a specific task and, once it was complete, was free to do as he or she wished with the remaining time. The task system promoted division of labor by gender. Female slaves were typically responsible for the rice crop: planting, weeding, harvesting, and processing. Men were responsible for the infrastructure around them: building canals and maintaining the water in the rice fields.

FREE TIME

Whatever the crop a plantation focused on, after 12 to 15 hours of work – longer at harvest time – slaves were allowed to return to their cabins. The evening was a chance to prepare a supper from the rations handed out every week. Slaves were usually given a combination of cornmeal, flour, lard, molasses, and a little meat. Vegetable patches or gardens offered a little variation and extra nutrition. Using these basic ingredients, slaves might prepare a cornmeal pancake for breakfast and a basic supper.

The main meal of the day was prepared in a kitchen by the cook, usually an elderly slave who was no longer able to toil in the fields. The food was served when the field slaves were given a lunch break. It was simple fare, typically some form of stew. Few slaves were overweight, many suffered from conditions like scurvy and rickets as a result of their poor diet.

Aside from eating, time at the cabin gave slaves a chance to meet with family and friends. For parents who toiled in the fields, it was the only chance to see their children. Older women tended to stay behind and look after children who were too young to work. Babies who needed to be breastfed would be taken to their mothers two or three times a day. Children were often unclothed until they reached working age. Adults were given a new set of clothes every year, typically at Christmas. The elderly benefitted from extra clothing to help them through the cold nights of winter.

Slaves on plantations formed communities. Owners were usually happy about this since slaves who formed close bonds were thought to be less likely to rebel or run away. Men and women were allowed to wed in informal ceremonies but the marriages were not legally binding, making it easier to split up families.

Any children born to a slave couple would themselves be slaves. Child mortality was high due to the poor conditions in the cabins, but those who survived were put to work as soon as they were old enough. Early tasks included carrying water to the slaves working in the fields or helping to mind the younger children. By seven or eight, enslaved children took their place alongside the adults in the fields. There was no education. Slaves were barred from attending schools and many states passed laws forbidding them from learning how to read and write.

Some slave owners banned their slaves from church services, too. Aware that the teachings of the Christian church did not always support the institution of slavery, the owners were keen that slaves did not interpret the teachings of Jesus as being in favor of equality.

IN THE OWNER'S HOUSE

Field slaves were often allowed Sundays off outside harvest time, but this privilege did not extend to slaves who provided help in the domestic setting. Slave owners were unwilling to manage on their own for one day a week, so slaves entered the plantation house as nannies, cooks, launderers, gardeners, cleaners, and servants. Many of these house slaves had better living and working conditions. They sometimes had access to better food – often the leftovers from the slave owner's table – and were given cast-off clothing. Some were even provided with a rudimentary education, despite the teaching of slaves being illegal.

Close proximity to the slave owner also brought its own challenges, since slaves were exposed to the whims of the owner and their family. Harriet Jacobs, a house slave from North Carolina, recalled her mistress "would station herself in the kitchen, and wait till it was dished, and then spit in all the kettles and pans" to stop the cook eating the scraps. House slaves who made mistakes were beaten. Female slaves were often raped by male members of the household.

Slaves tended to live in rudimentary log cabins with a single room for living and sleeping

The planting and harvesting seasons – in this case the planting of sweet potatoes – were busy times involving every able-bodied man and woman

Domestic slaves who worked in the plantation house might have had better conditions but faced their own challenges

This famous photograph showing the scarred back of Gordon, a slave who escaped during the Civil War, was widely circulated by abolitionists

All slaves, wherever they worked, were at constant risk of punishment. White overseers supervised the slaves as they worked, while drivers – themselves slaves who had been given extra responsibility – were just as feared. Both could be inhumanly cruel.

The primary form of control was the whip and club. Slaves could be flogged or beaten without mercy. So violent were these attacks that they were sometimes killed or maimed. Although it didn't benefit a slave owner's wallet if his property was no longer able to work, they thought it necessary to bully their workforce into maximum productivity. Mutilation and branding were also used as a punishment to scare an entire plantation into work.

Henry Box Brown remembered an overseer on the tobacco plantation where he worked: "On one occasion I saw him take a slave, and make him take him off his shirt; he then tied his hands and gave him 100 lashes on his bare back; and all this, because he lacked three pounds of his task, which was valued at six cents." Brown also recalled that slaves would be left to choke in the smokehouse if they incurred the overseer's wrath.

NOWHERE TO TURN

Slaves who suffered horrific punishments at the hands of their owners and overseers had no legal rights. A slave found guilty of crimes could be executed. The chance of a slave being declared innocent was low. Slaves did not have the right to give testimony in court against a White person. However, since a slave woman was the property of her master, a White man who raped her was guilty only of trespass. The vast majority of rapes were likely never reported.

The Southern states in which slavery was legal each adopted a slave code to restrict the rights of slaves. Although the specifics varied from state to state, the common idea was to keep the slaves under the tight control of their owners. Slaves were not allowed to own property but, as property themselves, slaves could change hands as the prize in a raffle or wager, be offered as security for loans, or be given as a gift.

Slaves could only seek comfort from within their community. Many sought to preserve the culture and traditions of their African homelands through oral history, music, and dancing. Although there were restrictions on their lives even here – drums were banned due to the fear that they could be used to send messages and signal an uprising – slaves danced in the evening and sang in the fields as they worked. As Frederick Douglass recalled, "The slaves would make the dense old woods, for miles around, reverberate with their wild songs, revealing at once the highest joy and the deepest sadness." The songs were a mournful reminder that, while their bodies were the property of their owners, their minds and souls strove to be free.

Urban slaves

Slaves in towns and cities were often skilled craftsmen but others labored in shipyards and factories

Although most slaves lived and worked within the confines of the plantations, there was life beyond the fence. In 1860, around 140,000 slaves lived in towns and cities. In Charleston, South Carolina, where the first shots were fired in the Civil War, a third of the city's population was enslaved.

Urban slaves tended to be skilled tradesmen and did not endure the same degree of physical toil as their brethren on the plantation. They plied their trade as tailors, butchers, masons, builders, and blacksmiths. Some learned their trades as apprentices. Others worked in shipyards, factories, and warehouses.

Sometimes they lived alongside their owners, often in an attic, back room, or outhouse. They were usually treated better than their plantation counterparts, not necessarily because urban owners were more humane, but because close proximity deterred owners from brutal punishments lest their own reputation suffer because of it.

Urban slaves were often hired out to bigger construction projects, during which living conditions would often deteriorate to dormitory-style housing approximating the shabby cabins found on plantations. However, a skilled slave individually hired out may have enjoyed greater independence. Some were given a small degree of control over their own affairs, including agreeing the conditions of their lease and retaining some of the fee.

SLAVE TRADE FACTS

Revealing some of the shocking statistics behind the horrors of the transatlantic slave trade

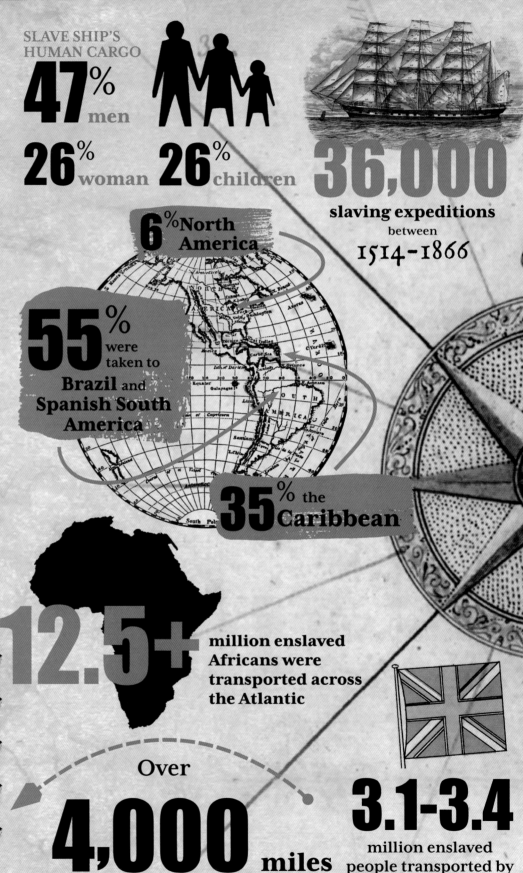

SLAVE SHIP'S HUMAN CARGO

47% men

26% woman

26% children

36,000 slaving expeditions between **1514–1866**

6% North America

55% were taken to **Brazil** and **Spanish South America**

35% the **Caribbean**

80 Days
the length of the journey from Africa to the New World

UP TO **16**%
of **slaves died** during **the Middle Passage**

12.5+ million enslaved Africans were transported across the Atlantic

Over **4,000 miles** the length of the Middle Passage

3.1-3.4 million enslaved people transported by **BRITISH SHIPS**

250-600

SLAVES PER BOAT

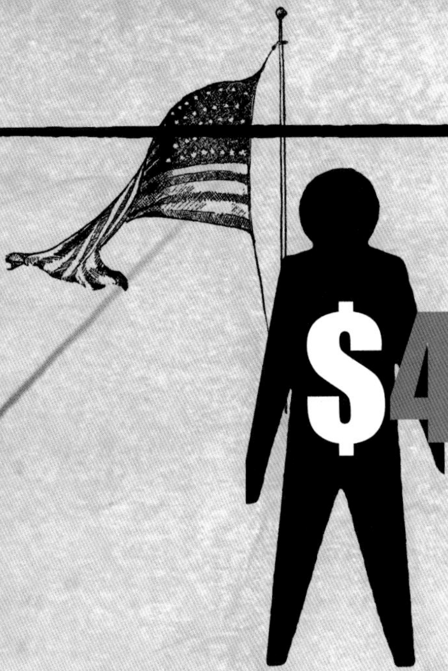

$40,000
average cost of a slave
in the American South in today's money

Black population in early America/United States

27,817 in 1700
757,208 in 1790
4,441,830 in 1860

3.9 million of whom were slaves

1/3 of newly arrived slaves would die within three years

Mortality rates were **twice as high among enslaved children** as among Southern White children

1/2
of all enslaved children died in their first year of life

£20 million
(*£17 billion in today's money)
compensation paid to British slave owners
following abolition in 1833

£0
compensation paid to the enslaved or their descendants since abolition

2015
The year **British taxpayers paid off the last installment of the bank loan used to compensate slave owners**

Images: Getty Images; Alamy (coffin)

IMPACT ON AFRICA

What became of those left behind, the family members and village-mates of the kidnapped enslaved who were shipped across the Atlantic?

Written by Arisa Loomba

I t is clear to many the impact that the slave trade had for Europe and the Americas, helping them to grow rich and to finance the Industrial Revolution. In Europe, a middle class began to emerge, enjoying greater leisure time, drinking tea and coffee with sugar, indulging in chocolate, exotic spices, fabrics, and stories of travel and adventure in foreign lands. In the Caribbean and Americas, we know that Indigenous people experienced unspeakable decimation and disease, almost wiped out as lush landscapes were broken into plantation land upon which African slaves harvested sugar, cotton, tobacco, rice, and many other crops that were quickly becoming essentials in Europe. But the story that is less well known, barely touched upon in comparison, is what was happening during this time in Africa while human beings were stolen on a daily basis.

West Africa had a rich history before European slavers arrived, with a complex political, economic, linguistic, and cultural landscape. Just like in Europe during this period, the balance of power was constantly changing. Wars were fought, kingdoms and dynasties toppled, city-states destroyed as new ones emerged. It is difficult to even categorize West Africa as a singular place, so diverse was it. Indeed, West Africans had been trading with Europe for centuries, via merchants in North Africa. The first European traders to set foot on African land were the Portuguese in the 15th century. Other European powers quickly began to follow.

There were four simultaneous slave trades occurring across Africa at this time. The Trans-Saharan trade saw people taken from the south, up through the Sahara Desert, and sold in Northern Africa. The Red Sea trade took people from inland and shipped them to the Middle East, and India. And the Indian Ocean trade included the sale of East Africans to the Middle East, India, and plantation islands across the Indian Ocean.

The Transatlantic slave trade, however, was, without a doubt, the most expansive, populous, systemic, and brutal of all. It marked a significant expansion of the African slave system from anything that had been seen before on the continent, as economies and ways of life began to

A mural depicting the capture of slaves

be structured around it. It was the largest long-distance coerced migration in history.

Before the slave trade became destructive and toxic, West African ports were dynamic and diverse marketplaces with goods sold from all over the world. Europeans wanted gold, ivory, and spices – mainly pepper. They kidnapped and traded Africans from the beginning, but it remained a small, fringe trade until the 17th century, when the demand for gold in Europe slowed. The slave trade boomed, replacing gold as the focus of commerce and becoming the dominant trade in the region. The impacts that this had on West Africa, and indeed the continent of Africa, as well as Europe and the Americas, is immense.

Sophisticated networks of trading alliances collected groups of people for sale. Often, these were people kidnapped or captured as prisoners of war in battle, or they were convicts sold away as punishment for crimes or to pay off debt. One

Bunce Island, in the Sierra Leone River, was run by the British commericial forms and was a major source of slaves

BANCE ISLAND, in the RIVER SIERRA LEONE.
The Property of John & Alexander Anderson Esq.ᵣ London.

A slavery fortress used to hold and guard captives before boarding ships, on Goree island, Dakar, Senegal

of the main commodities that the Europeans sold in return for slaves was guns and firearms.

The result of injecting metal guns and weapons into African society was devastating. Communities began using them as self-defense against both European slave traders and other African tribes and villages, who may attempt to wage war or steal their villagers to sell as slaves. A vicious cycle emerged, in which West Africans needed guns to prevent their village members from being captured and sold, but in order to buy guns, they needed to sell slaves. Thus, villages were constantly violently preying on and attacking one another to steal human beings. Much blood was shed.

Some kingdoms and city-states were decimated as a result of this. Others, like the Asante and Dahomey, grew rich and powerful. In Dahomey, which emerged around 1600, raiding for slaves was a way of life, inherent in the very founding of the state by the armed elite.

"A mentality emerged in which people felt they must either take or be taken"

This created huge rivalries and tensions between different states, and constant war reduced the possibility of political stability emerging. Ethnic fractionalization that continues to this day almost certainly has its roots in this period.

The slave trade was not a planned strategy to impoverish the continent; it was the result of centuries of participation in the trade on all sides. It is difficult and complex to try and understand the extent to which African societies were complicit in the slave trade and contributed to the sale and torture of human beings. There is much evidence to suggest that many African states, such as Angola, strongly resisted becoming involved in the economic system of trading in

slaves. Africans often damaged slaving vessels and rose up in revolt and rebellion against the system.

However, as the trade eclipsed every other in value, it became impossible not to. It was either sell slaves or get left behind. Those that didn't join in would become impoverished. A mentality emerged in which people felt they must either take or be taken. With a whole economic system built on the sale of human flesh, it is less a question of complicity than of need and survival, of ordinary people and everyday lives turning as small cogs in an epic system.

But it seems to be that African societies without a state or government were less prone

Images: Seylou Diallo/AFP via Getty Images (Goree Island); Alamy (Bance Island, mural)

to violence and raiding. Those with chiefs and a prominent elite would be targeted by the Europeans and influenced, offered rewards and wealth in return for slaves. Their sons were sent to Europe to study, and the nature of statehood changed. So much so, at the time of abolition, many African chiefs were dismayed. They did not wish to see the end of an industry that was their main function and source of wealth. This is one of the reasons that the Europeans were so keen to find alternative goods to trade in Africa other than slaves after abolition, particularly oil. It would allow them to keep African chiefs in a state of indebtedness and dependency. Africans were not so much partners, but servants and facilitators of the European slave trade.

"African states became deeply dependent on selling human beings"

The slave trade fundamentally changed the demographic landscape of many parts of West Africa. Sometimes, entire villages were stolen or killed. Whole areas were practically emptied of their human presence. Scholars have determined that the region faced a sustained and consistent depopulation. According to historian Patrick Manning, by 1850, Africa's population was only half of what it would have been had the slave trade never taken place. This was compounded by deaths caused by diseases brought in by European imperialists such as syphilis, smallpox, typhus, and tuberculosis, to which Africans had little to no resistance having never encountered such illnesses before.

This depopulation and instability created a major global imbalance in the ability of West Africa to recover from the pilfering and plundering of its population. Once a thriving economic center, West Africa was being stripped dry, and the profits were setting Europe far ahead economically, where before Europe had been on a similar footing, if not even less economically developed. The African economic model at the time was labor and agriculture intensive, and required a large number of people to work the land. It simply could not thrive under so great a population loss, nor the reallocation of resources away from agriculture and towards slave raiding.

Evidence shows a relationship between areas in which greater numbers of people were taken as slaves, and lower rates of economic and social development, according to typical outward or Western markers of development. For instance, lower literacy rates still exist in Nigeria and Ghana, where the slave trade was particularly

Altered societies: Gender, class and ethnicity

A chain of slaves traveling from the interior to the coast

In places where only some were taken, a gender imbalance was created. More men were kidnapped, leaving behind women, who were seen as less useful. They remained to keep the village running, and came under huge pressure to rebuild, care for, and support their villages.

But there were suddenly too many women and not enough men to marry, and so in some societies, men began to take multiple wives in a practice known as polygyny. Tensions and instability emerged with these new lifestyles, and this practice actually decreased the fertility of women, compounding population stagnation even further.

It wasn't only women whose roles were changing and developing as a result of the trade; a new class of 'merchant princes' found they could become rich. The children of chiefs and kings, many of whom had either been granted a European education or were

of mixed race and could speak European languages, discovered a new niche.

Given their ambiguous place in society – Black but wealthy, educated and somewhat respected by the White men – these merchant princes could act as intermediaries and army commanders aiding the Europeans, and extract sizeable profits for themselves. Indeed, the slave trade opened up a wealth of new employment opportunities at all levels, with workers needed as porters, interpreters, guards, soldiers and peddlers.

But while this may seem like a positive outcome for the African peoples, in reality these jobs were only available for the privileged. Only a small number of African villagers were involved directly in servicing the trade. And yet the impact and scale of human loss inflicted on peaceful and innocent villagers is immense and unimaginable.

A Gambian mural depicting the slave trade

A mural showing bartering over the price of a slave in Ghana, West Africa

Western imagination as inferior, backwards, and worthy of enslavement. Racism as we know it today certainly did not begin with the slave trade: racialized thinking and classing people on the bases of physical characteristics has a long history. However, the role of a racial characterization of Black people in justifying and sustaining the legality of slavery, was crucial.

As the successful West African economic landscape fell further and further into disrepair as a result of all that was happening, Europeans chose to interpret this as evidence of African savagery, backwardness, and an inability to function successfully in contrast to the West. They interpreted Europe's enrichment from enslavement and extraction as proof of their superiority, while Africa remained outside of history and progress.

Over the years, it became natural to believe that Africa and its people have made no major contributions to history, no crowning achievements, no role in shaping our modern world. It was attributed to Africans' innate nature, rather than the path that history took. This unjust representation may be the biggest impact of all.

And what of the emotional toll? The trauma and loss experienced by people living in constant fear for centuries is likely to have greatly negatively impacted the overall mental health of the region, diminishing productivity and motivation. This is a trauma that will have been inherited through the generations. Studies and explorations of West African art and literature show that the constant fear of kidnap, survivor's guilt, and the importance placed on community and traveling in groups is still prevalent within the public consciousness of the region. The past endures and clues of this can be found in cultural forms, even if it is not preserved in written historical documents.

prolific. Other studies show that, ironically, areas of West Africa with particularly rugged and inaccessible terrains today perform better economically than those that are open or coastal. Enclosed and remote inland areas were more difficult to raid for slaves, and thus had lower rates of depopulation as the terrain hindered trade and protected vulnerable communities. Interestingly, everywhere else in the world, 'rugged' regions are generally more economically impoverished, but in Africa, the phenomenon is undoubtedly linked in some part to the history of slavery.

It was also easier to raid and kidnap slaves when the weather was cooler, as enslaved people were less likely to die of heatstroke, exhaustion, or other diseases, and less money had to be spent to keep them alive. Colder areas were more likely to see many people captured and sold. New data analyzing weather patterns at the peak of the slave trade show that areas with colder weather during those years are the poorest today. It seems that once again depopulation due to the slave trade continues to have a negative effect on modern African economies.

African states became deeply dependent on selling human beings and buying guns for survival. Although Africa did not experience official or direct colonial rule on the ground until the 1860s, the slave trade can be seen as imperial rule by commerce, taking its inceptions back to the 16th century. The slow impoverishing of Africa in these years paved a convenient way for the 'Scramble for Africa' that was to follow after slavery was finally abolished.

Coastal societies saw the greatest change, as previously quiet fishing and salt-producing villages suddenly saw the building of factories, forts, and holding prisons and new languages spoken. A region that once traded primarily

overland was now part of growing sea routes and networks, and small villages became globally recognized ports.

Of course, we cannot say that 500 years' worth of change in West Africa is attributable to the slave trade; change occurs as part of slow and complex processes in every society. Moreover, these impacts were not uniform. West Africa is a vast region, almost as large as the US, and some places were largely uninvolved with Europeans. One reason the impact of the slave trade in West Africa has been explored in so little depth compared to other places is the lack of reliable statistical evidence. Another reason is simple historical amnesia. Very few people have thought it a worthy subject to address.

And yet a major lasting impact is, of course, the construction of Black peoples in the

A 1772 map depicting the West African 'Slave Coast'

96

84

102

78

90

FIGHT FOR FREEDOM

Explore how the enslaved resisted their cruel captivity and how the inhumane institution of slavery was finally defeated

THE FIGHT TO END SLAVERY

*In the late 18th century, a small group of people
set out to change the world – and they did*

●———— Written by Edoardo Albert ————●

For almost all of human history and in almost every culture, slavery has been an accepted and normal part of life, sanctioned by the powerful and accepted by the public. Slavery was seen as normal. It's important to remember this when reading about the long struggle against it. While to us slavery seems an obvious evil and its abolition a moral necessity, this clarity is only a result of the successful campaign to abolish it.

Japan prohibited slavery in 1590, an act based upon the Buddha forbidding monks and nuns to own or receive slaves, and his teaching that slave trading is not a good life for lay people. The

other civilization where slavery was prohibited was Christian. By the Middle Ages, slavery had effectively ended throughout Europe. But the jolting expansion of European horizons that began at the end of the 15th century, the scramble for riches and the struggle between European powers, led to a re-adoption of slavery that continued for more than 200 years until its final abolition. With Western societies turning decisively against slavery, and their dominant economic and military positions in the 19th and 20th centuries, they were then able to impose an end to slavery and slave trading throughout most of the world.

But none of this would have happened without the determined efforts of small groups of people who often endured ridicule, calumny, and attacks from the rich, the powerful, and the fashionable. It cannot be emphasized too strongly: slavery as an institution is normative throughout human history. The abolitionists were aiming to change the world.

Within the context of the New World, the first man to argue against slavery as an intrinsic evil was a Dominican friar. Bartolomé de las Casas was one of the first Spanish settlers on the Caribbean island of Hispaniola, where he entered the Dominican order as a friar in 1523.

and then priest. A witness of the appalling abuse suffered by the Indigenous people at the hands of Spanish settlers, las Casas forswore the slaves he originally owned and campaigned for the humane treatment of the Indigenous population, bringing his argument to the king, Charles V, Holy Roman Emperor.

Las Casas spent almost all his adult life arguing against slavery and the ill treatment of native peoples, being a principal speaker at the Valladolid Debate in 1550, which was the first European debate on the ethics and morality of colonization and the treatment of native peoples. In his efforts to protect Native Americans, he

initially advocated importing African slaves instead, but he later abrogated this view, writing: "The cleric [Bartolomé often wrote in the third person], many years later, regretted the advice he gave the king on this matter – he judged himself culpable through inadvertence – when he saw proven that the enslavement of Blacks was every bit as unjust as that of the Indians."

British ships and merchants became the major drivers of the Atlantic slave trade in the latter part of the 17th century and through the 18th century, leading to a huge expansion of trade and vast profits for merchants, ship builders, bankers, and their backers. Minor

ports, such as Bristol, Liverpool, and Glasgow, became major cities through the triangular trade that saw British manufactured goods exported to Africa, where they were exchanged for slaves, who were then transported to the Caribbean and North America, and sold for sugar, molasses, cotton, and tobacco, which were then shipped back to Britain.

The scale of the economic realignment of the country during the course of the 18th century is shown by the fact that in 1700, 82 percent of British exports went to Europe but by 1800 this had fallen to only 21 percent, while 61 percent went into the Atlantic economy that linked

Africa, the Caribbean, and North America. What's more, exports quadrupled during the century. These Atlantic exports sailed from Bristol, Liverpool, and Glasgow, turning them into rich and important cities. With so much money being made, and the slave trade generally going on out of sight and mind, initially there were few voices raised against the trade.

However, in the second half of the 18th century, people began to question the morality of the slave trade in Britain. In North America, the rhetoric of freedom underlay the rebels' case for fighting the American War of Independence. In France, 'Liberté, Egalité, Fraternité' was the slogan that overthrew the Ancien Régime. Indeed, inspired by their motto, the French revolutionaries abolished slavery throughout France and her dominions in 1794, only for Napoleon to reinstate the institution in 1802.

In Britain itself, slavery had been abolished by William the Conqueror, who outlawed the practice of selling prisoners of war that had been the custom of the Anglo-Saxons. But with the expansion of the Atlantic slave trade, some slave owners started bringing domestic slaves with them when they sailed back to Britain.

In 1772, this came to court in the case of Somerset vs Stewart. James Somerset, a slave, had been brought to Britain by his master, Charles Stewart, but escaped. However, Stewart recaptured Somerset and, imprisoning him, took him onto a ship intending to ship Somerset back to Jamaica and sell him. However, Somerset had been baptized while in London, making contact with abolitionists, who served a writ of habeas corpus questioning the legality of Somerset's imprisonment and proposed export. The case

A young William Wilberforce; he was 29 when he sat for this portrait and he would spend the rest of his life fighting slavery

"Faced with opposition, the abolitionists also sought to change the views of the public"

came before Lord Mansfield, who judged:

The state of slavery is. . . so odious, that nothing can be suffered to support it, but positive law. Whatever inconveniences, therefore, may follow from a decision, I cannot say this case is allowed or approved by the law of England; and therefore the Black must be discharged.

Although the exact legal ramifications of the judgement are still being discussed by scholars today, the English public took the ruling to mean that no man might be a slave on English soil. Hearing of the case, in 1778, Joseph Knight, an African slave brought to Scotland by his master, John Wedderburn, left Wedderburn and petitioned the courts for his freedom. Wedderburn, in the case of Knight vs Wedderburn, averred that Knight owed him 'perpetual servitude' but the Scottish Court of Session ruled that, under Scottish law, chattel slavery was not permitted and that furthermore slaves in Scotland could leave their masters and refuse to be sent back to slavery in the colonies.

Sniffing a threat to their wealth, British sugar merchants, planters, and colonial agents established the London Society of West India Planters and Merchants in 1780 to advocate for slavery and the slave trade. They had the money but the abolitionists were growing in fervor and numbers, while their arguments increasingly chimed with the spirit of the age.

With the general recognition that slavery was illegal in Britain, people became increasingly aware of how British merchants, bankers, shipbuilders, and mariners profited from the transatlantic slave trade – and the recognition hurt. In 1774, John Wesley, the founder of Methodism, wrote *Thoughts Upon Slavery* in which he vehemently criticized the institution. In 1776, clergyman Humphry Primatt wrote: "The White man (notwithstanding the barbarity of custom and prejudice), can have no right, by virtue of his color, to enslave and tyrannise over a Black man." And in 1785, poet William Cowper wrote:

We have no slaves at home.—Then why abroad?
And they themselves once ferried o'er the wave
That parts us, are emancipate and loos'd.
Slaves cannot breathe in England; if their lungs
Receive our air, that moment they are free,
They touch our country and their shackles fall.
That's noble, and bespeaks a nation proud
And jealous of the blessing. Spread it then,
And let it circulate through ev'ry vein

The American Revolutionary War was fought in the name of freedom but it left the slave population of America still in chains

Of all your empire. That where Britain's power
Is felt, mankind may feel her mercy too.

It was a truly remarkable change of sentiment and it brought a concomitant commitment to bring about change. On May 22, 1787, 12 men founded one of the most influential societies in history, the Society for Effecting the Abolition of the Slave Trade. Of its dozen founders, nine were Quakers, reflecting the prominent role taken by the denomination in the new movement, and three Anglicans, notably Thomas Clarkson, who had at this time already become a full-time campaigner against the slave trade, and Granville Sharp, a lawyer who had acted for slaves petitioning for their freedom.

Earlier that same year, Clarkson had also met the young MP William Wilberforce. Fired with the zeal of his conversion to Christianity, Wilberforce came to see that the mission Clarkson put before him was what God wanted of him. Writing in his journal, he said: "God Almighty has set before me two great objects, the suppression of the Slave Trade and the Reformation of Manners." In a country that

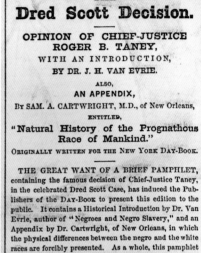

The Dred Scott decision of the US Supreme Court is generally held to be the worst decision in its judicial history, plunging the country into civil war

Olaudah Equiano
or
GUSTAVUS VASSA
the African

Published March 1. 1789 by G. Vassa

Olaudah Equiano was one of the founders of the Sons of Africa, an abolitionist movement of former slaves, and his autobiography was a bestseller, helping to change public attitudes before the abolition of the slave trade

had suffered civil war over religious divisions a century before, religious enthusiasm was mocked and derided but inspired by their faith, Wilberforce and the campaigners of the Abolition Society brought motion after motion before Parliament, calling for abolition.

Faced with opposition and delay in Parliament, the abolitionists also sought to change the views of the public, enlisting writers, painters, and poets in their cause. The Society printed pamphlets, published books, and organized lecture tours, with the talks often being given by freed slaves such as Olaudah Equiano and Ottobah Cugoano. Other anti-slavery organizations soon formed, including the Sons of Africa, a society of former slaves that campaigned for the abolition of the trade.

In 1807, 17 years after the first bill had been presented to Parliament, An Act for the Abolition of the Slave Trade received royal assent having been passed in the House of Commons by 283 votes to 16. The Act outlawed the trade in slaves within the British Empire although it did not outlaw slavery itself. It stipulated that

A slave station being fired on by sailors from the Royal Navy's West Africa Squadron after Britain had outlawed the Atlantic slave trade

This 1787 medallion produced by Josiah Wedgwood became hugely popular. Wedgwood, a close friend of Thomas Clarkson and an ardent abolitionist, donated hundreds to the movement

Under the Fugitive Slave Act, American slave catchers could apprehend escaped slaves even in the Northern free states

"The divide between the Northern 'free' and the Southern 'slave' states was deepening"

captains caught transporting slaves would be fined up to £100 for each slave found on their ship (about £9,500 in today's money). With slave ships carrying up to 500 people, it was a serious punishment. To back it up, the government dispatched the West Africa Squadron to patrol the coast. During its 52 years patrolling, the Royal Navy intercepted about 1,600 ships and freed 150,000 enslaved Africans.

However, slavery was deeply embedded in the Caribbean and elsewhere, and the end of the Atlantic slave trade did not bring about the withering away of slavery that Wilberforce and

his fellow campaigners had expected or hoped for. In 1823, the Society for the Mitigation and Gradual Abolition of Slavery Throughout the British Dominions, known as the Anti-Slavery Society, was formed, with many of the original campaigners, including Wilberforce and Clarkson, as founding members. The Society campaigned for slavery itself to be outlawed, although its members were split between gradualists, who favored a staggered end to slavery, and more radical members, who viewed slavery as a mortal sin that caused death to the soul. The Society continued the successful

campaigning tactics of its antecedent, publishing the first memoir from a female slave, *The History of Mary Prince, A West Indian Slave*, and in 1833 Parliament passed the Slavery Abolition Act.

Over in America, however, it would take more than passing a law to end slavery. During the American War of Independence, both British loyalists and American patriots promised freedom to slaves who fought on their side. But despite the Revolutionary army being between one-fifth and one-quarter Black, the new Constitution of the United States required free states to return escaped slaves to slave states. Already, the divide between the Northern 'free' and the Southern 'slave' states was deepening. By 1804, every Northern state had outlawed slavery, while the economy of the Southern states was becoming tied ever more closely to slavery, in particular following the invention of the cotton gin.

In the face of what Southerners came to call their 'peculiar institution', a growing abolitionist movement spread in the Northern states. Quakers were prominent early

Harriet Tubman was one of the leading abolitionists in the United States and helped lead slaves to freedom via the Underground Railway

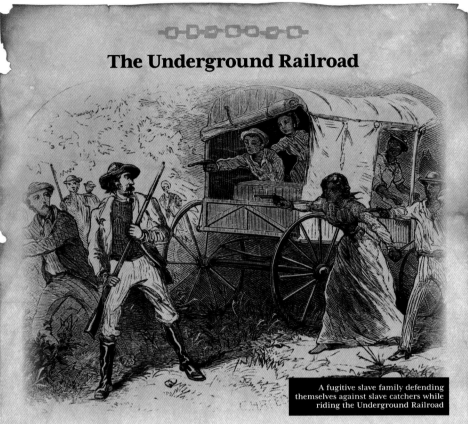

The Underground Railroad

A fugitive slave family defending themselves against slave catchers while riding the Underground Railroad

There were slave catchers in the American South, made fat and wealthy by claiming the bounty slave owners paid for the return of escaped 'property'. To get away to the Free States or Canada was like escaping from prison, with slave catchers and a hostile Southern population all around.

To help slaves get to freedom, abolitionists and escaped slaves developed the Underground Railroad, which was neither subterranean nor a railway but a clandestine network of routes, agents, safehouses, and helpers all committed to helping slaves escape.

The railway metaphor developed from the imperative to secrecy, with routes called lines, safehouses called stations, and helpers called conductors. The escaping slaves were called either passengers or packages.

Between 40,000 and 100,000 slaves were helped to freedom by the Underground Railroad. Perhaps the bravest of its conductors were people like Harriet Tubman, former slaves, who infiltrated back into Southern plantations to lead bands of escapees to freedom. If they were caught, the least they risked was re-enslavement.

opponents of slavery, and they formed the core of the first abolitionist society, the Society for the Relief of Free Negroes Unlawfully Held in Bondage, founded in 1775 and renamed the Pennsylvania Abolition Society in 1784. No less a figure than Benjamin Franklin became its president.

However, political power in Congress was evenly split between 'free' and 'slave' states, with 11 states in each camp. But as the United States spread westward, and new territories petitioned to be admitted to the union, the question of whether these new states would be 'free' or 'slave' states became ever more pressing. When Missouri asked to join the union as a slave state, a compromise was effected whereby Maine simultaneously became part of the United States as a free state, maintaining the uneasy balance. But the Missouri Compromise also stipulated that any future states north of the line of latitude at 36 degrees and 30 minutes would be free states, while those to the south of it would be slave states, extending slavery westwards with the same North/South divide.

A further effort at a solution was made in 1854 when the Kansas-Nebraska Act allowed that whether new states should be free or slave should be decided by a popular vote. Many politicians, seeing this as an effort by the slavery-supporting Democratic Party to expand the 'peculiar institution', left the party to join the new anti-slavery party, the Republicans.

Then, in 1857, the Supreme Court made its infamous Dred Scott decision, which declared that the descendants of Africans imported into America as slaves could not be American citizens. Moreover, the federal government had no power to outlaw slavery in new territories that were being acquired with the US's westward expansion. Thinking to end the political debate over slavery by making it a matter of settled law, the Supreme Court's decision had the opposite effect, and the Democratic Party split in two.

In 1860, Abraham Lincoln of the Republicans, the new abolitionist political party, took advantage of the Democrat split and was elected president. In response, Southern slave states withdrew from the Union, forming the Confederate States of America on February 4, 1861. There would be no more talking. The great moral question of America's founding would be answered in blood.

Images: Alamy except medallion

Frederick Douglass
SLAVE TO STATESMAN

Discover the remarkable rise of an agitator, reformer, orator, writer, and artist

Written by Arisa Loomba

Frederick Bailey was most likely born in February 1818 (although there are no records to prove the exact date) in his grandmother's slave cabin in Talbot County, Maryland. He was probably mixed race: African, Native American, and European, as it's likely that his father was also his master. His mother was sent away to another plantation when he was a baby, and he saw her only a handful of times in the dark of night when she would walk 12 miles to see him. She died when he was seven.

Frederick was moved around and loaned out to different families and households throughout his childhood. He spent time on plantations and in the city of Baltimore, a place he described as much more benevolent towards enslaved people, where they had more freedom and better treatment than on plantations. Indeed, Baltimore was one of the most bustling harbor cities in America, a meeting place of people and ideas of all kinds from all around the world; a place in which dreams and visions of freedom could easily be fostered.

One mistress, Sophia Auld, took a great interest in the 12-year-old, teaching him the alphabet. But her husband Hugh greatly disapproved of teaching slaves to read and write, believing it would equip them to access ideas and aspirations beyond their station. It would make them rebellious. Eventually, Sophia came to agree with Hugh's disapproval and herself believe that teaching slaves to read was wrong. She ceased her lessons and hid his reading materials, snatching newspapers and books from the enslaved boy's hands when he was caught with them.

Douglass was taught to read by his master's wife, Sophia Auld, but her husband convinced her to stop as he opposed teaching slaves literacy

This picture shows Douglass fleeing barefoot from two mounted pursuers with dogs

But Frederick was shrewd and continued to find ways to learn, trading bread with street children for reading lessons. He learned to buy knowledge and words from a young age. The more he read, the more he gained the language and tools to question and condemn slavery, developing his sense of Black identity and personhood for himself. When he was hired back out to a plantation owned by William Freeland, Frederick set up a secret Sunday school where around 40 slaves would gather and learn to read the New Testament. Surrounding plantation owners gradually came to know of these clandestine meetings and one day descended on the group armed with stones and clubs, permanently dispersing the school.

Not long after, Frederick was sent to work for Edward Covey, a poor farmer with a dreadful reputation as a 'slave breaker'. He was sent to

Anna Murray-Douglass, Douglass's first wife of 44 years, was known as a patient, loyal, and caring woman

be broken, to have his rebellious spirit crushed and be transformed into a docile, obedient worker. He faced frequent whippings, and at just 16 he resolved to fight back, physically asserting his strength over Covey. Frederick tried to escape once but failed.

That was before he met Anna Murray in 1837. Anna was a free Black woman in Baltimore who was five years older than him. The pair quickly fell in love and she encouraged him continuously to escape and find freedom, helping him to realize that freedom was truly within his grasp. The following year, in 1838, aged 20, Frederick made his break from the shackles of slavery.

He made the passage from slave state to free state in under 24 hours, boarding northbound trains, ferries, and steamboats until he made it to Philadelphia in Pennsylvania, then a Quaker city with a strong

anti-slavery sentiment. He then traveled to New York disguised in a sailor's uniform. He faced many close shaves, even catching the eye of a worker whom he knew, and who mercifully remained silent about seeing him. On setting foot in the North, Frederick was a new man, master of his own destiny. He was free to decide the direction of his own life for the first time, a thrilling and overwhelming prospect. Murray joined him up north, where they were quickly married and could now decide on their own name. They tried out Johnson, but eventually decided on Douglass. Settling in abolitionist stronghold towns in Massachusetts, they played active roles in a church community populated by many prominent former slaves, including Sojourner Truth and later Harriet Tubman.

By 1839 Douglass was a licensed preacher, a role in which he honed his speaking skills. He was also an active attendee of abolitionist meetings and developed strong friendships with campaigners like William Lloyd Garrison, who wrote the weekly newspaper The Liberator. Aged 23, Douglass gave his first anti-slavery speech at the Massachusetts Anti-Slavery Society Convention in Nantucket, and began touring across the country with fellow abolitionists. His

Constitutional contestations

A deep split in the abolitionist movement reveals the complexity of Douglass's vision and ideology

Historian David Blight refers to Frederick Douglass as one of the most critical readers, as well as speakers and writers, of the time. This is in reference to Douglass's radical reading of the US Constitution and the conflict it caused between himself and fellow abolitionist William Lloyd Garrison. Garrison believed that the US Constitution was an exclusive, elitist text that did not hold a place for the abolition of slavery or provide a legal or moral precedent for abolition. In this sense, the US was constitutionally, fundamentally, intrinsically pro-slavery, a bleak thought for abolitionists to accept. In demonstration of his disgust at this, Garrison burned a copy of the Constitution.

At first, Douglass agreed with Garrison's reasoning. However, he later became influenced by Lysander Spooner's publication of *The Unconstitutionality of Slavery* in 1846. This bolstered Douglass's idea that the Constitution did not support slavery, and slavery was not enshrined in the very idea of America's nationhood. The Constitution could and should be utilized as a tool to justify abolishing slavery, and was a document with good intentions that had been corrupted and misused. This caused Douglass and Garrison to break apart their partnership in 1847. It was the greatest notable split in the American abolition movement.

Douglass's understanding of how slavery was or was not bound up with the concept of the nation is seen by many historians as significant for its sophistication. Later, at the dawn of the Civil War, Douglass held great appreciation for Abraham Lincoln's insight that slavery could only be abolished if the nation – the Union – was violently fought over and won on the premise of being a free, non-slaveholding country, creating a fresh start. Douglass was both radical and conservative, imagining the violent upheaval of his world to make space for a new reality, but in which the tools of the current world could be invaluable.

He knew that America could only exist free of slavery if it underwent a major transformation, yet he also campaigned fervently against the popular idea of 'colonization', which suggested that slaves should be freed and sent to the Caribbean or back to Africa. Douglass saw that African-Americans had to have a stake in building this new nation and deserved to fight and defend their freedom, and he convinced Lincoln to allow African-Americans to serve in the Union Army. Though the US denied the humanity of slaves, Douglass did not seek to deny the US as his nation, nor see it as necessary to remove Black people in order to achieve freedom. Instead, Black people must themselves have a hand in building it. He was American and believed that America could be fundamentally redesigned to include and accept him.

rapid ascent from slave to celebrity took place over little more than one year.

As one of the few men to have escaped slavery with a willingness and ability to be so eloquent about his experiences, Douglass became a living embodiment of the impacts of slavery and an image of Black stature and intellect; a vision of what African-American people could become. He was used by White abolitionists to oppose general stereotypes of

from Britain's abolition movement of the early 19th century, such as Thomas Clarkson. It was during this time that Douglass finally gained legal freedom and protection from recapture, with English acquaintances raising the funds to officially buy his freedom from his master Thomas Auld. The public endorsement Douglass received from influential figures in Europe only increased his credibility in the States. He returned with £500 donated by

> ## "Douglass became an example, a living embodiment of the impacts of slavery, and an image of Black stature and intellect"

African-Americans as ignorant or lazy. In some ways, Douglass became like a zoo animal on display, a success story trophy, and he knew it. This strained his relationships with some other major abolitionists, like Garrison. Nevertheless, Douglass also recognized the power of challenging and reshaping harmful caricatures of Black people and began to take hold of and manipulate his own representation in speeches, writing and images.

Douglass spent two years touring Ireland and Britain between 1845 and 1847, lecturing and meeting with the last remaining abolitionists

English supporters and used it to set up his first abolitionist newspaper, *The North Star*. Alongside this, he and his wife were active in the Underground Railroad, taking over 400 escaped slaves into their home, offering them rest and safety on their journey to freedom.

Douglass was an advocate for dialogue and alliances across ideological divides. Notably, he was a supporter of women's suffrage campaigns and attended many events in favor of the cause, such as the Seneca Falls Convention, at which he was the only African-American present. Though he faced a backlash for his contribution, it was

Douglass appealing to President Lincoln and his cabinet to enlist Black men

Images: all Alamy except Getty Images (pen)

A photographic pioneer

Photography was a major part of Frederick Douglass's belief system and his efforts to defeat slavery and racism

At a time of great social change in the 19th century, photography was quickly growing as a new art form. With the invention of daguerreotypes, it was increasingly cheap and accessible, and Douglass saw it as a democratic medium that could serve the needs of the people. He considered that whereas politicians could lie, peddling false images and caricatures of slaves to justify slavery's continuation, the camera would tell the truth. Nuanced, serious, sophisticated images of Black people portrayed as human beings rather than property could challenge negative images, particularly blackface and minstrelsy.

Douglass was the most photographed American of the 19th century (even more than Abraham Lincoln!), a remarkable record for a Black man and ex-slave. Around 160 images of him have been found, taken over many years. He stared directly into the camera, confronting the viewer, and never smiled. Typically, the sitter would be asked to stare softly into the distance or look beyond the camera, and to smile. But Douglass's stare holds a challenge to be taken seriously – he did not want to present himself as a smiling, happy, obedient slave. Simultaneously, he played into other trends recognizable to the eyes of White viewers as dignified, educated, wealthy, and accomplished; his formal dress and swept-back hair took on the attributes of a classical hero.

His portraits were reproduced as lithographs and engravings and distributed to promote his talks. His use of photography was subversive and highly political, reflecting his sophisticated political philosophy, his understanding of how public opinion was formed and influenced by the media, and his belief in the social power of art.

A rare photograph of Douglass with his second wife, Helen Pitts Douglass

only after Douglass's speech that a resolution was passed in favor of female suffrage, indicating his power as an orator. But his interaction with the cause was controversial, because not everyone was in favor of women's rights. Many believed African-American freedom, equality, and suffrage was the far more pressing and urgent issue, and that Douglass's endorsement only gave more power to White female voters, who would vote against Black people's interests.

But Douglass was more astute than this. Indeed, Richard Bradbury argues that, bolstered by his tours through Ireland and Britain, he connected the struggle against slavery with many other issues: poverty in newly industrialized London, Irish famine and Home Rule, and women's rights. In his later years as a statesman, Douglass even engaged with Caribbean and Latin American ideas about multiculturalism and democracy in challenging white supremacy. And he was interested in issues affecting Native Americans and recent immigrants. He was American, through and through, but he also looked beyond the nation that had enslaved him and legally rejected him as a fellow man and citizen, towards the international stage. This gave him a space to

construct and consider what he stood for and enter into dialogue with those in a like-minded pursuit of change. This global, cross-struggle outlook has helped to make Douglass such a modern, sympathetic figure, with communities across the world claiming him for their own. He created a greater sense of a united class of downtrodden people who could together overthrow their common oppressor through coordinated efforts.

One of Douglass's chief arguments, as illustrated in his famous *What to the Slave is the Fourth of July?* speech of 1852, was the importance of education in improving the lives and opportunities for African-Americans. He was an early advocate of school desegregation, building upon his early experiences teaching at his Sunday school as a slave. He was also a deeply religious and spiritual man and believed that Christianity did not endorse slavery. Douglass chose to abstain from alcohol, tobacco, and other 'corrupting' substances to keep his body 'pure'. Like many involved in struggles against oppression who took divine inspiration, from Thomas Paine to Nat Turner, to Elizabeth Cady Stanton, he saw himself as a prophet heeding God's will.

This contemporary print places Douglass as a highly distinguished and central figure of both racial politics and American politics at large

sight for the US to annex as an additional state to relieve racial tensions by providing African-Americans with their own state. Later, in 1889, President Harrison appointed him as the US minister resident and consul-general to Haiti, and the chargé d'affaires to Santo Domingo. So popular and influential did Douglass become in the top echelons of American politics that he became the first African-American to be nominated for vice president of the United States (though without his knowledge or approval) in 1872.

This latter part of Douglass's life was turbulent. Though he was highly revered and favored, there were, of course, critics and he was often in danger. His home was at one point burned down in an arson attack, causing him to move to Washington, D.C. with his family. A disagreement with radical abolitionists caused him to flee into exile abroad. His family life also became a focus of gossip and scandal: he had two affairs with White women while his wife Anna was alive. She died in 1880, and Douglass remarried two years later to a White suffragist and abolitionist 20 years his junior, Helen Pitts.

> "He created a greater sense of a united class of downtrodden people who could together overthrow their common oppressor through coordinated efforts"

Douglass published three versions of his life story, in 1845, 1855, and 1881 (with a revised edition in 1892). Each autobiography, written at different stages of his life and career, have different tones, aims, and ideological outlooks. By the time of the American Civil War in 1861, Douglass was one of the most famous Black men in America. He was both an ardent supporter, and honest critic, of Abraham Lincoln and his approach to ending slavery. Later, during the Reconstruction era, Douglass went on to receive several political appointments, such as becoming the President of the Freedman's Savings Bank.

During a violent period of backlash against newly emancipated slaves, and the rise of the Ku Klux Klan, Douglass supported Ulysses S. Grant in his 1868 presidential campaign to combat segregation and violence. Grant sent Douglass on a mission to the West Indies and Haiti, leading him to work with the US government on issues related to the Caribbean and its potential. Grant wanted to see if Santo Domingo could be a good

His affairs and controversial second marriage tainted Douglass's reputation. Indeed, later accounts written by his children (Douglass had five), indicate that the real saint may have been their mother, who remained Douglass's most ardent supporter, protecting his name and retaining the dignity and respectability required of women at the time, despite her husband's affairs and absences. Shockingly, despite Douglass being one of America's most revered writers and intellectuals, his first wife remained illiterate all her life.

Douglass continued touring and traveling, speaking and campaigning into his final days – literally to his very last moments. After receiving a standing ovation for a speech on women's suffrage in 1895, the 77-year-old Douglass collapsed with a heart attack. Thousands passed by his coffin to pay their respects, and he continues to be honored by countless statues, remembrances, and plaques across the globe. He is remembered for his understanding that agitation, education, work, and reform were the crucial areas in which change could transform the lives of African-Americans, and America as a whole.

A statue of Douglass in the US Capitol's Emancipation Hall in Washington, D.C.

In 1831, America's slavers' worst nightmare was materialized in the form of Nat Turner's Southampton Revolt, tearing the abolition discourse wide open

REVOLT AND RESISTANCE

From the dawn of the transatlantic slave trade, the forces of enslavement and oppression were met with an undercurrent of revolt and resistance

Written by Hareth Al Bustani

Between the 16th and 19th centuries, more than 12 million African men, women, and children were captured and shipped across the Atlantic to the Americas, to slave away for European and Euro-American planters. However, from the earliest days, revolt and rebellion were entrenched deep within the DNA of the transatlantic slave trade.

It began in Africa, where villages and towns established fortifications and warning systems, to deter attacks from traders and enemies. As slave ships pulled away from the continent, free Africans continued to attack them from the shore. Those who were unable to escape should not be considered passive observers to their fates; for free-hearted people living in captivity, their entire existence was a series of acts of revolt and resistance.

Though most had no idea what fate lay in store for them, the journey across the Middle Passage gave enough of a glimpse. Conditions on the slave ships were so atrocious that up to one fifth of those hauled across the Atlantic perished before even reaching the Americas. As a result, one in ten journeys were interrupted by some form of insurrection. Between 1699 and 1865, there were more than 50 large mutinies, and almost 500 cases of violent insurrection against more than 360 slave ships. The slaves aboard the ship Clare not only revolted, but successfully overthrew the crew from the ship, liberating themselves and landing at Ghana's Cape Coast Castle. When violence proved futile, though, slavers would often make a cruel example of the rebels, by executing them on full display of neighboring vessels. However, some poor

The ever-increasing restriction on their rights forced slaves to develop systems of evasion and resistance, transforming congregation or worship into acts of rebellion

souls chose to simply commit suicide instead, by jumping overboard or starving themselves, preferring to die free, rather than live as slaves.

SUBHUMAN STATUS

Those who survived the journey across found themselves auctioned off to predatory cash crop plantation owners, to whom they were merely tools to achieve profit maximization. Despite superficially identifying with Christian values, and the American and French Revolution notions of all men being created equal, planters warped their personal ethics to fit their business interests. Under their paternalist worldview, Black people were considered subhumans, who must be made dependent on their owners – or as one racist Louisiana plantation owner wrote, "Inspire a Negro with perfect confidence in you and learn him to look to you for support and he is your slave." Managing the power dynamics between slave owner and slave was precarious, and having emerged from a history of rebellion,

Slave mutinies were so commonplace that one in ten slave ships traveling the Middle Passage were rocked by revolts, and even mass suicides

"Those who dared to revolt were burned alive, hanged, or starved"

planters were always keenly aware of the potential explosive power of the collective slave populace.

Slaves were habitually overworked and underfed, forced to live in crowded dirt floor shacks, and denied basic human rights. Although laws and conditions varied from region to region, they generally had no right to acquire property or earn wages, making them totally dependent on their masters for basic sustenance. Their owners, meanwhile, only provided them enough to keep them alive and working. To make sure they were squeezing every ounce of productivity from their workers, planters either used overseers to keep slaves in line, or relied on a slave driver – slaves who were given greater privileges in return for brutally punishing anyone deemed unruly, or unproductive. Slaves were beaten and tortured daily, often to death, and might find their wives and children sold off to another owner without warning.

For slaves, simply holding social meetings and church services constituted great acts of rebellion. This oppressive way of life naturally developed a perpetual counterstream of evasion and resistance. In its simplest form, slaves often feigned illness, started fires, 'accidentally' broke tools, or simply tried to flee – all of which caused significant financial losses to their masters.

Denied the right to meet in groups, they kept meetings secret, sending lookouts to track patrols, and even leading militia into dead ends or booby traps when necessary. Some might keep a store of hot ash and coal ready to be thrown out in case they were discovered, buying themselves time to escape.

THE POWER OF THE POWERLESS

Despite the slavers' best efforts, a powder keg can only be shaken so much before it explodes. When England seized Jamaica from Spain in 1655, many slaves fled inland and established free communities in the thick forests of the Cockpit Hills, from where they launched regular guerrilla attacks on plantations. The repercussions were severe; those who dared to revolt in Barbados and Antigua were burned alive, hanged and even starved to death.

Having endured a rebellion led by White colonist Nathaniel Bacon, Virginia was particularly paranoid about the spirit of insurrection spreading to the Black slave populace who, in some counties, were as numerous as White farmers. The state passed several laws, banning large meetings between Black people and preventing them from wielding weapons, while banning slaves from leaving their masters' property without permission.

However, it was the French colony of Saint Domingue, home to 500,000 slaves – the Caribbean's largest slave population – where tensions between planters and slaves boiled over. The island's overworked, underfed slaves produced a third of the world's sugar, making it the richest colony on Earth. Desperate to maximize profits, planters forced slaves to wear

White abolitionist John Brown's failed attempt to spark a slave revolt played a major role in accelerating the coming Civil War

tin masks to keep them from chewing sugar cane in the fields, and regularly whipped them, before rubbing hot ash and salt into the wounds.

For the emerging class of educated, more prosperous freemen of color like Vincent Ogé, these conditions contradicted France's alleged commitment to the Declaration of the Rights of Man. In 1790, Ogé traveled to France to campaign for universal voting rights for Black people, but was flatly rejected. After returning, when the local governor also refused to remove racist restrictions, Ogé tried to stir up a revolt, but was convicted of treason. He and another rebel had their arms, legs, hips, and thighs smashed with hammers, and were then tied to wheels and left to bake to death in the sun, before having their heads cut off and stuck on pikes.

In France, this barbaric treatment evoked disgust against the colonialist planters, and the National Assembly granted citizenship to all people of color born to free parents across the colonies. But for Saint Domingue's slaves, this was nowhere near enough. The next year, a group of slaves rose up in revolt, setting fire to the instructions of their enslavement and

Early American revolts

In 1741, when a series of fires broke out across New York and Long Island, a witch-hunt saw dozens of slaves hanged and burned

Rooted in a history of White-led revolt and rebellions, the state of Virginia was absolutely terrified at the prospect of a slave revolt. In 1687, the governor of Westmoreland County had his worst fears confirmed when he received word of the country's first suspected Black slave-led insurrection. Desperate to put a stop to other slaves getting the idea of rising up, he set up a special commission to try and execute the suspected conspirators as quickly as possible. In the aftermath, further laws were passed, allowing legal authorities to kill any slave who dared to resist their masters, run away, or refuse to surrender. Englishmen were also prohibited from marrying anyone who was not White.

Half a century later, in 1739, a slave named Jemmy led 100 Angolan slaves on a killing spree across the Stono River region towards St Augustine, Florida, where they would be free under Spanish law, beating drums and chanting, "Liberty." Gathering Black recruits and burning down White houses, they fought for a week, killing 20 people, before being suppressed by the English – inspiring a series of subsequent revolts. Two years later, when a series of fires broke out across New York and Long Island, it was blamed on a joint slave-Catholic conspiracy, sparking a witch-hunt. Despite little evidence, up to 40 slaves were hanged or burned at the stake, alongside four Whites, and many more were exiled.

The stunning victories of Saint Domingue's slaves over two of the world's pre-eminent superpowers, Britain and France, sent shockwaves across the world

murdering hundreds of White Europeans. The insurrection sent shockwaves across the aristocracy of Europe, and France soon realized this revolt would not be put down as easily as those that had come before. In just two months, the rebels burned down hundreds of plantations and seized the north of the colony, under the leadership of Toussaint L'Ouverture.

Over the ensuing decade, the rebel slaves first fought against France, and then allied with them against Britain and Spain, once the French abolished slavery. In 1801, having made peace with Britain, Napoleon sent the largest ever French invasion force to the island and captured L'Ouverture, but was utterly routed, losing 50,000 men in the process. Three years later, having defeated two of the world's pre-eminent superpowers, the island declared independence, establishing the Republic of Haiti, and bringing an end to three centuries of slavery. It was an unprecedented moment; one that sent a simple message to every slaver and slave across the New World; all bets were off.

RIPPLES OF REVOLUTION

Among those in America inspired by the Haitian Revolution was a literate blacksmith slave, known as Gabriel Prosser, who planned to raise 1,000 slaves in revolt, beneath the banner of 'Death or Liberty' – only to be betrayed and executed. Yet another was Charles Deslondes – a slave-driver of Haitian descent, who carried out his duties with terrifying diligence. The last person anyone would expect to lead a rebellion, his reputation provided a perfect cover for his revolutionary activities.

On January 8, 1811, Deslondes led 500 slaves along River Road, burning plantations down towards New Orleans, where he hoped to link up with more revolutionaries. Armed with copies of the French Rights of Man, which they had long hidden in their quarters, and experience of fighting in Ghanaian and Angolan civil wars, the rebels knew their only options were freedom or death. Dressed in military uniforms, riding on horseback, they cut a powerful image, one that White New Orleans would not soon forget. Although the rebels were far closer to achieving their goal than any would care to admit, after two days of fighting they ran out of ammunition. When Deslondes was captured, rather than being placed on trial, he was tortured and killed. Later, 95 of his followers were executed, and their heads mounted on pikes, running 60 miles along River Road, a stark message to any would-be rebels.

ALL ROADS LEAD SOUTH

By the 19th century, thanks to the invention of the cotton gin, the American cotton industry, centered in the Deep South, exploded, becoming the country's leading export. As profits soared, so too did demand for slaves, and after the

Toussaint L'Ouverture was leader of one of the most successful slave rebellions, which saw hundreds of plantations burnt down in Saint Domingue

international slave trade was abolished in 1808, Upper South states like Virginia gained a stranglehold over the country's domestic slave market. However, the Deep South cotton supply grew so large it sent the global price plummeting, sparking a depression that blocked up the domestic slave market, leaving Virginia with a huge slave population. By 1820, two fifths of Virginia's one million residents were slaves, with 1.5 million more across the South.

In 1829, Governor John Floyd warned that there was a "spirit of dissatisfaction and insubordination" among the country's slaves, and a minor media sensation accompanied the acquittal of a Black man, Jasper Ellis, accused of "promoting an insurrection of the slaves." Still desperate to maintain total control, Virginia's 101,488 militia members patrolled at night; whipping anyone caught roaming around without a pass. By now, White slave owners had long-established a system of brutality, designed to keep their 'property' living in perpetual terror.

One slave who was caught trying to escape had a chain clamped so tight around her leg, it developed an infection, which stripped all the flesh from the bone. When another woman went into labor and collapsed from exhaustion, her overseer whipped her so violently she died, and her daughter was born with lashes on her back. Another still was whipped so badly, she remarked to her friend, "Fannie, I don' had my las' whippin'. I gwine to God," and killed herself.

In 1830 and 1831, America's leading abolitionists met at the Negro Conventions to propose creating a college for Black people. However, Virginia legislature banned free Black people from congregating for the purposes of education, marrying Whites, or living with slaves, and sold all Black criminals into slavery.

TURNER'S REVOLT

In this crucible of oppression and cruelty, a slave called Nat Turner fomented a revolt that would shake America to its core. Turner was born a Southampton slave in 1800; his mother was a slave but not much is known about his father. As a young boy, Turner began having

---

> "In just two months, the rebels burned down hundreds of plantations"

In 1831, a prophetic slave named Nat Turner embarked on a violent killing spree, hoping to spark a wider revolution among America's slaves

The power dynamics of slavery created the twin forces of brutal control, exercised by the oppressors, and bold resistance from the slaves

religious experiences and after learning to read and write, became convinced he was a prophet receiving messages from God, coded in visions and signs in nature. When Turner perceived a "loud noise in the heavens," as a solar eclipse and atmospheric phenomenon coincided, he was convinced he must rise up in bloody revolt.

On August 21, 1831, he and some followers went into his master's house and killed the entire family. They spent the next day-and-a-half sweeping from one plantation to the next, liberating slaves, taking weapons, and murdering every White person in sight. They eventually grew to 50 strong, killing almost 60 White people, before being put down by the local militia. Turner himself remained on the run for six weeks – in which time, White America was consumed by hysteria. White planters abandoned their land and hid their families in the forest, as rumors of further insurrections spread like wildfire. When a second rebellion, involving 25 slaves, hit North Carolina, the paranoia spilled over, as White volunteers rode across the South, indiscriminately torturing and murdering Black Americans. Some newspapers even celebrated the most prolific murderers and in Georgia, militia captains tied slaves to trees and hacked them to death.

After being caught in a swamp by a hunter, Turner faced execution. His corpse was flayed and his flesh and bones turned into souvenirs. However, his revolt had dragged the issue of slavery to the forefront, and the Virginia legislature was soon overwhelmed with petitions;

ranging from the emancipation of Black slaves, to the deportation of free Black people to Africa. A fierce debate on January 25, 1832 concluded that while most believed slavery was evil, none were willing to foot the bill of abolition. Virginia and its neighbors doubled down, banning Black people from meeting in groups after 10 p.m., preaching without a license, owning arms, attending their own religious services, learning to read, selling food or tobacco, and buying alcoholic spirits.

GROWING UNREST

In the ensuing decades, abolitionism grew into an increasingly divisive movement. Tensions boiled over in 1859, when the White abolitionist John Brown famously led an attack on the arsenal at Virginia's Harpers Ferry, joined by just 21 men. Brown hoped to break into the mountain town's arsenal, seize its 100,000 guns, and use the success to instigate a massive slave rebellion.

Despite the overwhelming odds, he was so sure of the moral imperative of the revolt that he took three of his sons on the raid. However, the attackers were promptly surrounded by marines, led by Robert E Lee, and Brown himself was taken captive. Afterwards, he was hanged, making him a martyr and a household name. While awaiting death, he wrote, "I, John Brown, am now quite certain that the crimes of this guilty land will never be purged away but with blood." Fairly soon, the entire country would be drenched in blood with the American Civil War, in which Brown's memory would serve as an enduring flame of inspiration for the abolitionist Union army. From the ruins would arise the hope of long-overdue emancipation for America's slaves, who had for so long risked it all resisting their brutal captivity, knowing that freedom would one day come.

Aftershocks

The Haitian Revolution inspired scores of rebellions across the region, such as Barbados, which had seen more than a century of peace. Although the British eventually put the insurrection down, killing 1,000 and executing 214; slaves from 70 plantations had come together to destroy a quarter of the islands' sugar cane. Despite the brutal retribution, slave revolts continued to grow in size and sophistication, to the point where the Caribbean experienced two a year.

When Britain's Parliament finally began to debate abolition, Jamaica's planters violently rejected any notion of emancipation, creating a climate that bred yet another slave insurrection, known as the Baptist War. Launched shortly after Christmas Day in 1831, it saw up to 60,000 of the island's 300,000 slaves rise up in revolt. The rebellion was launched by Samuel 'Daddy' Sharpe, a preacher who drew inspiration from other recent revolts across the Caribbean. What began as a strike soon snowballed into mayhem. However, although it was eventually quashed, Britain came to the decision to adopt full emancipation across its colonies just years later.

In Brazil too, dozens of uprisings broke out, centered on the sugar, cotton, and tobacco-rich region of Bahia, culminating in the Malê Revolt in 1835, where 600 African Muslim slaves and freedmen battled with cavalrymen, police, National Guard, and militia men for three hours. It was a major stepping stone on the long path to Brazilian emancipation, which was finally formalized in 1888.

The success of the Haitian slave revolt inspired several similar insurrections across the Caribbean and beyond, for decades to come

THE WAR TO END A 'PECULIAR INSTITUTION'

The United States, in its modern form, came to birth in blood: the struggle over a principle: that one man may not own another

— Written by Edoardo Albert —

Slavery – and the struggle to outlaw the practice – defines the history of the United States as much as the earlier War of Independence. But there should be little surprise that slavery was practiced in America, for it has been a universal human institution, carried out throughout history and in pretty well every civilization. What is unusual about slavery in America was that it eventually became the great political, moral, and religious issue of its day. America baptized itself in blood over a principle: that no man might own another.

During the American War of Independence, both British loyalists and American patriots promised freedom to slaves who fought on their side. But despite the Revolutionary army being between one-fifth and one-quarter Black, the new Constitution of the United States required free states to return escaped slaves to slave states. For already the divide between the

Northern 'free' and the Southern 'slave' states was deepening. By 1804, every Northern state had outlawed slavery, while the economy of the Southern states was becoming tied ever more closely to slavery, in particular following the invention of the cotton gin.

In the face of what Southerners came to call their 'peculiar institution,' a growing abolitionist movement spread in the Northern states. Quakers were prominent early opponents of slavery, and they formed the core of the first abolitionist society, the Society for the Relief of Free Negroes Unlawfully Held in Bondage, founded in 1775 and renamed the Pennsylvania Abolition Society in 1784. No less a figure than Benjamin Franklin became its president.

The framers of the Constitution, aware of the tension between 'free' and 'slave' states, had deliberately balanced political power between the two groups, with equal numbers of states

belonging to both camps. It was a compromise that was inevitably tested as the US expanded. When new territories asked to join the Union, each admission threatened the status quo. When Missouri became one of the United States in 1821 as a slave state, the balance was maintained by simultaneously admitting Maine as a free state. The Missouri Compromise sought to extend this balancing act westwards. North of the line of latitude at 36 degrees and 30 minutes, territories admitted to statehood would be free states; south of that line would be slave states.

The problem with the Compromise was that it had no mandate from the people living in the new territories. With slavery an evermore contentious issue, a fresh effort was made to embed the status of new states as free or slave by letting the people decide by vote. The 1854 Kansas-Nebraska Act, intended to provide this popular support, caused the slavery-supporting

In Ulysses S Grant, President Lincoln finally found a general to win the war for the Union

Black soldiers of the 107th Colored Troops stand outside their guard house at Fort Corcoran

General Robert E Lee, the Confederate general whose great military ability almost brought victory to the South

Despite the prospect of being executed or re-enslaved should they be captured, Black Union soldiers fought bravely during the Civil War, earning their place on the front line

'40 acres and a mule'

An ambitious attempt to give restitution to former slaves failed in the aftermath of Lincoln's assassination

There were some 3.9 million Black slaves in the South. Following the end of the Civil War, and the end of slavery, how were they going to support themselves? One suggestion was that the vast plantations owned by the White slaveholders of the South should be parcelled out to their former slaves, both in reparation for their unpaid labor and to provide for their future.

The policy was first promulgated by General William Tecumseh Sherman in his Special Field Order No. 15 on January 16, 1865 following his discussions with 20 leaders of the Black community in Savannah, Georgia. The order stated: "The islands from Charleston, south, the abandoned rice fields along the rivers for 30 miles back from the sea, and the country bordering the St Johns river, Florida, are reserved and set apart for the settlement of the Negroes now made free by the acts of war and the proclamation of the President of the United States."

The policy, which became known as '40 acres and a mule,' had an electrifying effect in the South. Freedmen throughout the former Confederate states hastened to claim the land and found self-governing settlements. However, on April 15, 1865, Abraham Lincoln was assassinated. His vice president, the Democrat Andrew Johnson, succeeded and overturned the order, returning the land to its original owners: the plantation slaveholders whose revolt had precipitated the Civil War in the first place. The long tale of efforts to forestall the emancipation of America's Black citizens had begun.

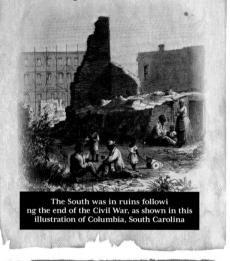

The South was in ruins following the end of the Civil War, as shown in this illustration of Columbia, South Carolina

"Black soldiers played a vital part in the final years of the war"

Confederate artillerymen lying dead beside their cannon after the Battle of Antietam

Democratic Party to split, with many leaving to join the anti-slavery Republicans.

With the issue of slavery continuing to divide the nation, the Supreme Court decided to bring what seemed an intractable debate to an end by settling the question in law. In 1857, the Court handed down its notorious decision in the Dred Scott case, which judged that the children of people taken from Africa as slaves could never become American citizens and that the federal government did not have the authority to make slavery illegal in the country's new Western territories. Far from ending the debate, the decision enflamed matters further.

With the Democratic Party split, Abraham Lincoln, the candidate for the abolitionist Republican Party, won the presidential election in 1860. With the 'peculiar institution' the Southern states considered essential to their prosperity under threat from the new government, the slave states formed the Confederate States of America on February 4, 1861. The talking was over. The abiding moral question of America's identity, whether it be free or slave, would be settled by war.

At the outset, it seemed the war would be over quickly. The Union greatly outnumbered the Confederacy, while also having a vast advantage in manufacturing capacity as well as many more miles of railroad. However, the states of the Confederacy had a much stronger martial tradition and some particularly able military commanders, as well as shorter internal lines of communication and a coastline that was so long that the Union strategy of naval blockade, to starve the South of needed imports, could not be strictly enforced. And while the Union fought for a principle, the soldiers of the Confederacy generally fought for more immediate and personal reasons: the defense and preservation of their way of life and institutions, particularly slavery.

These immediate advantages enjoyed by the Confederacy were shown in stark relief at the first major battle of the Civil War: the First Battle of Bull Run on July 21, 1861. Expecting

an easy victory, and under intense public pressure to march on the Confederate capital, Richmond, Virginia, Union forces were stopped and turned back by Confederate troops just north of the city of Manassas, which lay 30 miles southwest of Washington, D.C. Forced to retreat, panicked Union troops routed and fled back to Washington. It was an ill omen.

Realizing the war would be long and bloody, both sides called up fresh drafts of recruits. In contrast to the dash of the Confederate generals, the men initially put in charge of the Union Army were cautious, so it was not until the spring of 1862 that General George McClellan authorized a fresh advance into Confederate territory, taking Yorktown on May 4.

However, counterattacks led by the Confederate generals Robert E. Lee and Thomas 'Stonewall' Jackson at the end of June pushed the Union Army back. By the end of August, the Confederate forces were moving on to the offensive, launching their own invasion of the North. However, the Battle of Antietam on September 17, the bloodiest single engagement of the war, stopped the Southern advance, although winter then brought a pause to the war.

But while winter stopped the military efforts, it did not stop the conflict at the political level. Following the Union victory at Antietam, President Lincoln issued the Emancipation Proclamation, stating that from January 1 all enslaved people in the Confederate states "shall be then, thenceforward, and forever free." Having signed the Proclamation, Lincoln said, "I never in my life felt more certain that I was doing right than I do in signing this paper."

While the Proclamation applied to the Confederate states in revolt, and therefore had little practical effect, it was hugely important symbolically, elevating the ending of slavery to a war aim as important as defending the Union and ensuring that Britain and France,

The executive committee of the
Pennsylvania Anti-Slavery Society in 1851

A watercolor (c1863) by Henry Louis Stephens of
a Black man reading the newspaper account of
the Emancipation Proclamation

President Lincoln visiting General
McClellan and other Union officers
during the Battle of Antietam

both intensely anti-slavery countries, would not provide support to the Confederacy. The proclamation also made it possible for Black Americans to serve in the Union forces and, by the war's end, some 200,000 men did so. Shortly before his death, Lincoln said of the Proclamation: "It is my greatest and most enduring contribution to the history of the war. It is, in fact, the central act of my administration, and the great event of the 19th century."

While the Union now accepted Black soldiers, the majority of them escaped slaves from the Southern states, it was initially reluctant to arm them properly or put them into the front rank of battle. However, the excellent performance of Black companies – the Union Army remained segregated – meant that Black soldiers played an increasingly vital part in the final years of the war, despite the grave risks that they ran should they be captured. The Confederates regarded Black Union soldiers as traitors and rebels, either re-enslaving or executing them if captured.

As for the war, 1863 saw a series of bloody battles that ground down the Confederacy's reserves of manpower. In 1864, Lincoln finally found a general, Ulysses S. Grant, to match the fighting spirit, and outmatch the competence, of the Southern commanders. Together with General William Tecumseh Sherman, he fought a war of attrition against the South, wearing down its ability to sustain and wage war until, finally, on April 9, 1865, General Robert E. Lee surrendered at the Appomattox Court House in Virginia. The American Civil War was over. The first war of the industrial age, its casualties – currently estimated at about 750,000 soldiers and that number again of civilians – presaged the killing fields of the Great War.

With Abraham Lincoln, the architect of victory, dead following his assassination on April 15, 1865, the aftermath of the war left open the question of how to bring together the exhausted combatants. The period that followed, the Reconstruction, would become one of the great lost opportunities of American history.

A CELEBRATION OF EMANCIPATION

An engraved illustration by Thomas Nast from 1865 celebrates the emancipation of Southern slaves following the end of the American Civil War. Images on the left highlighting the cruelty of slavery and life under the Confederacy contrast with Nast's portrayal of a somewhat optimistic vision of the future for freed Black Americans on the right. However, for many Black Americans in the South, emancipation would not mean the end of their struggles as discrimination and racism continued.

PATION.

PUBLIC SCHOOL.

CASHIER.

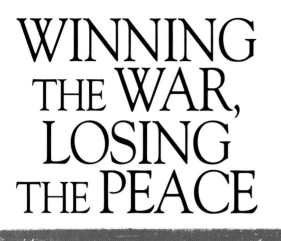

WINNING THE WAR, LOSING THE PEACE

After the war came Reconstruction, but for many Black Americans the struggle continued

Written by Edoardo Albert

S lavery was over. The Union had been saved. The great question of principle that had divided the nation had been settled, in blood. There could be no going back after so many lives had been lost. And in Abraham Lincoln, America had a leader with the wisdom, insight, and compassion to heal the nation while ensuring the principle over which the war had been fought – the emancipation of the enslaved – would not be lost sight of. But then, on April 14, 1865, five days after General Robert E. Lee's surrender brought the Civil War to an end, Lincoln and his wife went to see the play Our American Cousin at Ford's Theater in the capital. While they watched the play, actor and Confederate sympathizer John Wilkes Booth crept up behind the couple and shot Lincoln from close range in the back of the head. Fatally wounded, Lincoln died eight hours later. Booth himself escaped but was shot dead two weeks later. Lincoln had won re-election in November 1864, so his vice president, the Southern Democrat Andrew Johnson, was sworn in to take Lincoln's place with almost a full four-year term ahead of him.

KEEPING THE STATUS QUO

Unfortunately, President Johnson was as committed to racism as he was committed to the Constitution. Being a constitutionalist, he made sure the Southern states had the freedom to govern themselves. Being a racist, this freedom allowed the recently Confederate states to pass a series of laws intended to put the newly freed slaves back on the plantations and to keep them there.

In the immediate aftermath of the war, Johnson, using his presidential powers, offered pardons to all the White citizens of the Confederate states save the leaders of the Confederacy and the major plantation holders, who had to petition personally for pardon.

An engraving from 1867, showing freedmen voting for the first time in New Orleans

Election campaigns sought to portray the Freedman's Bureau, a federal organization protecting freed Black slaves, as a ticket to idleness for "lazy" Black people

"New legislatures set about enacting laws that restored slavery in all but name"

Johnson also proposed returning all land and property to dispossessed Southerners, with the exception of their human property: slaves were not to be restored to their previous owners. The individual states also had to ratify the Thirteenth Amendment to the Constitution that outlawed slavery. In return, citizens of the South had to swear loyalty to the Union, and the states had to disavow secession from the Union and cancel the debts run up during the Civil War. They were generous terms, and it seems likely that Lincoln would have supported them. When asked by a Union general how to treat the defeated enemy, Lincoln had replied, "Let 'em up easy."

However, it's unlikely that Lincoln would have acquiesced in the way Johnson did when it became clear that the states were using the freedom they had been given to ensure that freed slaves were kept in a condition as close to slavery as possible. Johnson, the Southern Democrat, believed, "White men alone must manage the South". The new legislatures set about enacting laws that restored slavery in all but name: freedmen could only work as field laborers, Black men without work could be sold to planters to work as laborers and Black children could be taken from their families.

THE FIGHT CONTINUES

The Republican-dominated Congress reconvened in December 1865. Johnson had already declared that Reconstruction was over, to the horror of the Republicans who had fought for the emancipation of the slaves. What's more, many former Confederate officials had been elected to serve in Congress, including Alexander Stephens, the vice president of the Confederacy. However, when these Confederates presented themselves to Congress, the Clerk of the House refused to include them among the elected members.

In defiance of the Democrat president's obstructionism, the Republican Congress passed the Civil Rights Bill, which granted citizenship to all men "without distinction of race or color, or previous condition of slavery or involuntary servitude". However, presented with the Bill, President Johnson vetoed it. In defiance of the president, Congress voted to overturn Johnson's veto and the Civil Rights Act was passed into law on April 9, 1866.

In the South, the Ku Klux Klan was founded in Tennessee and increasing racial tension led to three days of rioting in Memphis, Tennessee, which saw 48 people, almost all Black, killed.

An increasingly radical Congress proposed the Fourteenth Amendment to the Constitution,

The Battle of Liberty Place, 1874, when White League militia attacked the racially integrated police force of New Orleans

THE LOUISIANA OUTRAGES—ATTACK UPON THE POLICE IN THE STREETS OF NEW ORLEANS

A cartoon by Thomas Nast, published in *Harper's Weekly*, highlighting the violence of white supremacist groups in the South

Ulysses Grant, commanding officer of the Union forces during the Civil War and 18th president of the United States

which defined a United States' citizen as simply someone born in or naturalized to the United States, and sent it to the states for ratification, with the demand that the states in the South ratify the amendment as the price of being readmitted to the Union. In the congressional elections of the autumn of 1866, voters returned a House of Congress full of radical Republicans determined to restart Reconstruction. Such was their majority in Congress that President Johnson could no longer obstruct their program. Congress proceeded to pass a series of Reconstruction Acts, dividing the South into five military districts under army control and forcing them to accept Black suffrage. This began what came to be called Radical or Congressional Reconstruction, which lasted to 1877.

During most of this period, the Republican Party controlled most of the Southern states. To enact the Reconstruction Acts, many Northerners came south – soldiers, teachers, and businessmen – who came to be called carpetbaggers after

their suitcases made from stitched-together carpet. On the South side, the locally born White Republicans were called scalawags, and were mainly small farmers. Finally, local Black people overwhelmingly voted Republican in an effort to end the racial segregation of the South and to gain some economic and political power. Black Americans were elected to Congress and the Senate, and many more served in state legislatures and as the everyday elected officials in the South, from sheriffs to justices of the peace. For a society that had based itself upon segregation, this Black emancipation came as a tremendous shock. For many White Southerners, it seemed that their Black slaves had suddenly become their political masters – and they weren't happy about it.

Through 1867 and 1868, most of the Southern states were readmitted to the Union (Georgia, the last, was readmitted in 1870) and, on July 9, the Fourteenth Amendment to the Constitution was ratified. President Johnson, who had escaped impeachment by the narrowest of margins (one

The vice president, Andrew Johnson, became president after Lincoln's assassination. He is often ranked among the worst presidents in American history

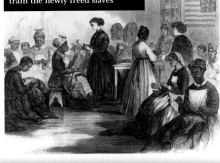

Many teachers from the North went to the South to educate and train the newly freed slaves

While denied political rights, Black churches became established in the South, serving as focal points for community life and hope

vote in the Senate, Congress having voted to impeach) was denied a shot at re-election by the Democrats, who chose Horatio Seymour, who had served as governor of New York, as their nominee for the presidential elections. For their part, the Republicans nominated General Ulysses Grant, the military architect of the Union victory in the Civil War. Grant won the election – although the margin was tight. It was the votes of newly enfranchised Black men that provided the Republicans with the necessary votes to win.

A LEGAL FIX

With a Republican president, Congress and Senate, legislators in Congress passed the Fifteenth Amendment to the Constitution, which stipulated that all men were entitled to vote, regardless of race, color, or previously having been a slave, and sent it off to the states for ratification. The amendment was a response to the increasing levels of violence in the South, where white supremacist organizations were trying to stop Black emancipation. The first among these was the Ku Klux Klan, which targeted freed Black slaves and Republicans with threats, violence, and murder. However, as reports of the violence reached Washington, Congress passed the Enforcement Acts, which allowed the federal government to protect the rights of Black citizens when their local legislatures failed to do so. The third of the Enforcement Acts, known as the 'Ku Klux Klan Act', which was passed in 1871, targeted the

Klan and by its effective application destroyed this first iteration of the Ku Klux Klan as an organization. However, local Democrats, seeking to overturn Republican rule, started similar organizations that served as the enforcement arm of the Democratic Party, eventually helping it to return to power in the South.

While Radical Reconstruction had begun with great idealism and high hopes, it was eventually tarnished as corrupt. Political scandals in the North served to taint many high officials, and rumors of the corruption of Black government officials in the South began to spread. While President Grant won re-election in 1872, patience and appetite for the Reconstruction was beginning to run out. The war had ended seven years earlier, and the attention of voters and politicians was turning elsewhere. Despite continuing violence in the South, the Democrats won the Congressional elections at the end of 1874, taking a majority in the House. By 1876, among the Southern states, only Louisiana, Florida, and South Carolina were under Republican control. With control of the House, and most Southern state legislatures, the Democrats began passing a series of racist laws and statutes that were collectively called the Jim Crow laws, ensuring continuing racial segregation in the South. These laws remained in place until 1963. While the Republicans, who had fought so long and hard for Black emancipation, won the war, it was the Democrats, with their dogged defense of white supremacy and racial segregation, who won the peace.

A new lynch mob

The massacre that showed how little things had changed

The 1872 elections in Louisiana were strongly contested and evenly split between Republicans and Democrats. In the aftermath, with rumors swirling of paramilitary groups taking control of local parishes, a Black militia force, led by the Civil War veteran William Ward, took control of the courthouse of Grant Parish in April 1873. As white supremacist forces gathered, Ward left on April 11 to seek help from the state governor. Two days later, white supremacist forces, armed with a cannon, opened fire on the courthouse. After a brief fire fight, the Black defenders surrendered. But in the aftermath of the surrender, a massacre took place, with somewhere between 60 and 150 of the Black militia being killed, many after they had surrendered and been taken prisoner. The massacre generated newspaper headlines throughout the country and federal forces eventually arrested 97 men for the crime. However, fearing that a trial for murder before a state court would see the accused's acquittal, they were charged with breaking the Enforcement Acts, rather than with murder. But when the case was appealed to the Supreme Court, the court found for the defendants, arguing that the Enforcement Acts only applied to states and not to

While the Colfax massacre produced national outrage, its outcome showed to Black Americans in the South that little had really changed: there was no redress

individuals. Thus the perpetrators of the massacre escaped unpunished.

For Black people in the South, there was now no redress against corrupt and biased local courts. With the passing of the first Jim Crow laws, the re-segregation of the South was in place.

Images: Getty Images (Grant, Johnson, Colfax Massacre)

118

108

114

LEGACY & IMPACT

Discover the lasting impact of the transatlantic slave trade on the United States and communities around the world

Throughout the 20th century, African Americans campaigned tirelessly to end racial inequality and segregation in the United States

THE LONG MARCH TO FREEDOM

After the Reconstruction, Black Americans gave their lives to overthrow a system of subjugation, persecution, and suffering, with dignity and courage

● Written by Hareth Al Bustani ●

For America's freed slaves, as the Reconstruction era came to a close, so too did the promise of everlasting liberty, equality, and peace. In the agricultural South, despite being promised '40 acres and a mule' each, freed families soon saw their land returned to its previous Confederate owners by President Andrew Jackson. With no opportunities, many were forced to become sharecroppers – a practice where landowners allowed them to work on their land in return for a portion of their harvest. Desperate to carve out a new life, scores of Black people migrated north and west to cities like Chicago, Detroit, New York, Philadelphia, and Los Angeles, only to encounter racism and hostility there, too.

Although the Thirteenth, Fourteenth, and Fifteenth Amendments had abolished slavery, provided citizenship, and guaranteed Black people the right to vote, the Supreme Court rapidly undermined this progress. In 1883, it ruled that while states could not discriminate against African Americans, citizens could – paving the way for the re-institutionalisation of racism via the Jim Crow laws, named after a racist minstrel song. These were not real laws ratified by the federal government, but a mosaic of state and local laws, codes and agreements that collectively restricted the rights of Black people. Although circumstances varied across the country, in many towns and cities, Jim Crow laws formalized a policy of segregation – separating Black and White people in all manners of life, from cradle to grave.

Black babies had to be born in Black hospitals, and Black corpses were buried in Black graveyards. Signs reading 'Whites only' and 'colored' were hung over bus stations, water fountains, toilets and building entrances, segregating every aspect of life, from recreational

The Jim Crow patchwork of laws, codes, and agreements were designed to keep Black people subjugated in poverty, away from the polls

After the abolishment of slavery, many Black people worked as sharecroppers – where landlords let tenants use their land, in return for a some of their produce

Between 1882 to 1968, 3,446 Black people were lynched by the Ku Klux Klan and other white supremacist hate groups

facilities and schools, to prisons and the armed forces. In 1896, the Supreme Court made yet another devastating decision, in the case of HA Plessy v JH Ferguson. Plessy, who was defined as an 'octoroon' – a person of one-eighth Black descent – argued it was unconstitutional for New Orleans to segregate public transport, but the Supreme Court disagreed. The decision birthed the 'separate-but-equal' notion; that it was perfectly acceptable for a state to segregate facilities and services, so long as they were equal.

It was even illegal for White and Black people to marry, and despite legally having the right to vote, Black people were prevented from doing so by the poll tax, fraud, literacy tests, and physical intimidation. Adding a further barrier, the 'grandfather clause' stipulated that no one

Segregation was just one method devised by racists to control and suppress Black people

could vote unless their grandfather had – an impossibility for the descendants of slaves.

A SYSTEM CREATED TO SUPPRESS

Jim Crow laws formed the pillars of a socioeconomic system designed to keep Black people subjugated in poverty. Despite being outlawed, many White employers practiced 'debt peonage' – where they would advance Black employees' money, and detract from their wages. Workers would often find themselves indebted to sharecropping planters, merchants, and company stores, trapped in a cycle of debt, working for free.

Those who managed to rise against all odds and obtain an education or professional proficiency, found themselves the victims of White envy and fear. From 1882 to 1968, 3,446 Black people were lynched by the Ku Klux Klan and other white supremacist hate groups, who burned down homes and killed with impunity – desperate

"Jim Crow laws formed the pillars of a socieconomic system designed to keep Black people subjugated in poverty"

to keep African Americans in a perpetual state of terror and, more importantly, away from the polls. When 17-year-old Jesse Washington was found guilty of raping and murdering a White woman in Waco, Texas in 1916, more than 10,000 people gathered to watch and participate in his prolonged torture and lynching – with children, the mayor, and police chief in attendance.

As Black people continued to seek opportunities in the country's industrial centers, by 1908, tensions were simmering. Though only 5.5 percent of its 47,000 residents were African American, Springfield, Illinois, was home to the state's largest Black populace. However, unlike European immigrants who competed for jobs in the factories and coal mines, Springfield's African Americans were largely confined to menial roles, as unskilled laborers, wagon drivers, shoe shiners, yardmen, furnace stokers, or servants.

That summer, as two Black men sat accused of unrelated sexual assault and murder charges against White people, a White mob surrounded the jail, calling for blood. When police smuggled

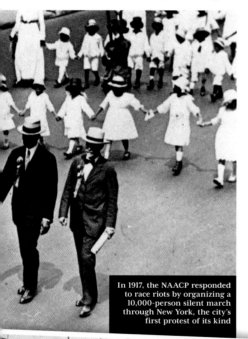

In 1917, the NAACP responded to race riots by organizing a 10,000-person silent march through New York, the city's first protest of its kind

In 1963, police in Birmingham, Alabama attacked peaceful protestors with dogs, fire hoses, and batons – bringing Southern racism to the world's attention

Massacre on Black Wall Street

After a foiled lynching, a bitter White mob burned down the US's most successful Black community, butchering hundreds along the way

White racists razed the affluent Greenwood District to the ground, killing hundreds and leaving 10,000 people homeless

By the end of World War I, Tulsa, Oklahoma, was home to one of the country's most affluent Black communities – centered around the Greenwood District, dubbed 'Black Wall Street'. To African Americans the community, with its own cinemas, banks, and hotels, was a beacon of hope. To the White community, it was a source of bitter resentment.

On May 31, 1921, the *Tulsa Tribune* ran an inflammatory piece, reporting that Dick Rowland, a Black man, had tried to rape a White woman. Before long, a White mob assembled by the courthouse, where the sheriff had barricaded Rowland inside. Worried that Rowland would be lynched, a group of Black supporters turned up, but before long shots were fired, and the Black group fled into Greenwood. Furious, the frenzied White mob chased after them, shooting Black people on sight, while burning down and looting buildings all across Greenwood.

As Black Wall Street burned, the governor declared martial law and sent in the National Guard, who, instead of arresting the rioters, interned all the city's 6,000 Black residents in the Convention Hall and Fairgrounds – some even joining in the carnage. After 24 hours of mayhem, behind the billowing smoke, the facts began to emerge: 35 city blocks razed; 800 people injured; hundreds of people killed; 10,000 left homeless.

Some residents remained interned for eight days, though the charges against Rowland were dropped. Many of the region's White residents and the American Red Cross offered a helping hand to the victims, but no one was ever prosecuted for the massacre. Instead, local authorities did their best to cover up the event; burying victims in unmarked graves, destroying police records, and removing the inflammatory *Tulsa Tribune* article before the microfilm transfer.

the two suspects out to safety, 5,000 angry rioters turned their rage on the city – burning down and looting Black businesses, before murdering and lynching two Black people, and killing several others. The *Illinois State Journal*, home to a racist comic strip mocking Black Springfieldians, blamed the Black community: "It was not the fact of the Whites' hatred toward the Negroes, but of the Negroes' own misconduct, general inferiority, or unfitness for free institutions were at fault." Tellingly, one of the targets of the riot was the saloon from which local Black political party leaders operated.

FORMING A VOICE

The riot paved the way for the creation of the Black advocacy group, the National Association for the Advancement of Colored People (NAACP). In 1917, the group's first president, Moorfield Storey, successfully argued before the Supreme Court that Louisville had violated the Fourteenth Amendment by forcing White property owners

into covenants where they could only sell to White people. Later that summer, when dozens of Black people were killed and thousands left homeless by an Illinois race riot, the NAACP organized a 10,000-strong silent march down New York's Fifth Avenue – the city's first protest of its kind.

It was a dangerous time. D.W. Griffith's acclaimed 1915 film *Birth of a Nation*, popularized Black stereotypes and idealized the Ku Klux Klan – whose membership would soon surge to three million. In the ensuing years, millions of Southern African Americans left for the North, and the emergent West. When the US entered World War I, more than 350,000 African Americans served in segregated units – with 1,400 eventually becoming officers, and three regiments awarded the Croix de Guerre for valor. As Black veterans returned home, they did so with their heads held high. Black sharecroppers were finally starting to earn more money, thanks to a surge in international demand for textiles. But this newfound confidence only further enraged White racists, who broke out

The power of education

Booker T. Washington and W.E.B. Du Bois may have had differing views, but both paved the way for equality in education

As the son of slaves, Booker T. Washington was born in 1856 without a family name. After the Civil War, he traveled 200 miles on foot to West Virginia, where, after enrolling at grammar school, he adopted his stepfather's forename of Washington as his surname. Having started work at the age of nine at a salt furnace, he went on to study at the Hampton Normal and Agriculture Institute, and then Wayland Seminary. Returning to Hampton, he was nominated the first principal of Tuskegee Normal and Industrial Institute in 1881.

In this role, he championed the education and empowerment of African Americans, encouraging Black people to pursue vocational skills in order to secure their constitutional rights. However, he was also dubbed 'The Great Accommodator' for suggesting that African Americans should "compromise" and accept segregation, while simultaneously contributing funds in secret to help combat the legal war against segregation.

W.E.B. Du Bois, who founded the collective of Black scholars and professionals known as The Niagara Movement, denounced this "compromise." Born free, he stressed the importance of Black people pursuing a classical education, and producing intellectual leaders to achieve social and political equality. In response to Washington's compromise, he penned *The Souls of Black Folk* – crafting an intellectual argument for the Civil Rights Movement to come.

A founding member of the NAACP, Du Bois helped to raise the bar of what Black people should expect of society, as well as their own self-image. After serving as editor of the NAACP periodical, *The Crisis*, for two decades, and consulting the UN founding convention, he moved to Ghana in 1961, dying at the age of 96 – just shy of the March on Washington.

Unlike Washington, Du Bois denounced segregation, and in 1945, spoke at the United Nations, calling for the abolition of colonialism

President Eisenhower had to send federal troops to Little Rock, Arkansas, in 1957, when the governor used the National Guard to stop nine Black students from attending an all-White high school

in 25 riots across the country in the 'Red Summer' of 1919, killing hundreds of people and burning down thousands of homes.

INCREASING RESISTANCE

As the US entered the 1920s, New York's Harlem neighborhood became a beacon of Black culture. Among its 175,000 residents were scores of scholars and artists, who drove a cultural explosion known as the Harlem Renaissance – a phenomenon mirrored elsewhere as far away as Cleveland and Los Angeles. Alain Locke, the Harvard-educated 'Dean of the Harlem Renaissance,' called it a "spiritual coming of age," that transformed "social disillusionment to pride." With a profound influence on American literature, theater, music, art, and dance, it gave Black people a platform to express the African-American experience. It was a Black man, Jesse Owens, after all, who dealt Hitler's white supremacist ideology a humiliating blow by becoming the first American to win four gold medals, at the 1936 Berlin Olympics.

In 1941, as Hitler rampaged across Europe, civil rights leader Asa Philip Randolph began organizing a 100,000-person March on Washington, demanding desegregation of armed forces. Keen to avoid the protest, President Roosevelt quickly acquiesced and issued an executive order eliminating discrimination in the defense industry. More than one million Black people would go on to serve in World War II, mostly in support units.

Following the war, although 1952 marked the first year the Tuskegee Institute reported no lynchings, the fight had only just begun. The NAACP's efforts to tackle the 'separate-but-equal' principle culminated in a landmark ruling in the case of Brown v Board of Education. After considering legal precedent, research on the adverse effects of segregation and the significant inferiority of schools Black people had to attend,

the Supreme Court ordered the desegregation of schools "with all due speed."

August 1955 marked one of the most notorious lynchings to date, when 14-year-old Emmett Till was tortured, killed, and thrown into a river for supposedly wolf whistling at a White woman in Money, Mississippi. His body was so disfigured he could only be identified by a ring on his finger, and his mother insisted on an open casket, to show what racists had done to her son. Although the world was appalled, the all-White jury acquitted the killers, who confessed their guilt to *Look* magazine the next year.

Among those who were sickened by the event was a 43-year-old Black seamstress, and long-time civil rights activist, Rosa Parks. On December 1, as she boarded a bus in Montgomery, Alabama, she recognized the driver as the same one that had kicked her out into the rain 12 years earlier. Riding the bus was stressful enough – after paying the fee, Black people were expected to board from the back door, and often the driver would take their money and then speed off before they had the chance. During the journey, when the driver told Rosa to get up and give her seat to a White passenger, she refused. For her trouble, she was arrested and fined $14. The incident sparked a citywide boycott, spearheaded by a young Southern Baptist minister, Dr. Martin Luther King

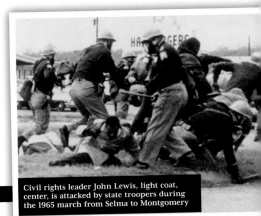

Civil rights leader John Lewis, light coat, center, is attacked by state troopers during the 1965 march from Selma to Montgomery

When Rosa Parks was arrested for refusing to give her seat up to a White person, the subsequent 381-day boycott resulted in desegregation of Montgomery's buses

Despite having different approaches, both Martin Luther King Jr, left, and Malcolm X, fought, and died, for Black rights

Jr. An earth-shaking orator, Dr. King emerged as the Civil Rights Movement's most prominent leader, and the first president of the Southern Christian Leadership Conference – devoted to nonviolent civil disobedience.

Dr King found himself at odds with Malcolm X, the most recognizable spokesperson for the Black nationalist group, the Nation of Islam, who advocated a more militant strain of activism – calling for self-sufficiency. Yet as the collective Civil Rights Movement gathered momentum, many Whites continued to resist desegregation. In September 1957, President Eisenhower had to send federal soldiers to Little Rock, Arkansas, to escort nine Black students to high school – because the governor used the National Guard to deny them access.

In 1958, in protest of the Oklahoma City's segregated lunch counters, a teacher and 13 Black students walked into a major drugstore and simply sat down, waiting to be served. Despite being asked to leave, they remained – even as racists punched, kicked, and spat on them. Two days later, an employee handed one of the children a hamburger, and before long, almost all

"Photos emerged of children and young people being clubbed and bitten by police dogs"

of Oklahoma City's stores and restaurants were desegregated. Sit-ins swept across the nation, and in Nashville, after an activist's house was bombed, the mayor admitted desegregation was wrong on the steps of City Hall.

LAWS VS REAL LIFE

Although the Supreme Court ruled it was illegal to segregate interstate travel facilities, when a group of Black 'freedom riders' put this to the test, they were attacked and one of their buses firebombed. Similarly, when Dr. King and the Southern Christian Leadership Conference led a peaceful protest through the segregated city of Birmingham, Alabama in 1963, they too were attacked – this time by the police. Photos emerged of children and young people being blasted by fire hoses, clubbed, and bitten by police dogs. Their dignity in the face of callous aggression struck a powerful chord.

Later that year, the Civil Rights Movement reached a crescendo, when 260,000 people descended on Lincoln Memorial for the March on Washington for Jobs and Freedom. There, looking out over a sea of White and Black supporters, Dr. King delivered his remarkable *I have a dream* speech. Momentum now snowballed towards John F. Kennedy's Civil Rights Bill – which his successor, Lyndon B. Johnson, supported. On July 2, 1964, after years of suffering, demonstrating,

marching, and sacrifice, Black rights were enshrined in law. Following much deliberation, capped by an 83-day filibuster, the Civil Rights Bill was passed, outlawing discrimination on the basis of race, color, religion, sex, or national origin, while guaranteeing equal access to public places, employment, and schooling.

The following year, after Malcolm X was assassinated, Dr. King led a campaign to win the right to vote in Selma, Alabama, by marching 54 miles from Selma to Montgomery. On one of the days, 500 marchers were attacked by state troopers and a mob, an incident televized nationally. By the last day, the march had grown from 600 to 25,000 people – prompting President Johnson to champion the Voting Rights Act, banning literacy tests and other methods used to disenfranchise Black voters, while appointing federal registrars to oversee elections. Between 1964 and 1969, the percentage of Black adults registered to vote rose from 35 percent to 65 percent. Another landmark case in 1967, Loving v Virginia, saw the Supreme Court force 16 states to overturn laws prohibiting interracial marriages.

In 1968, a week after the assassination of Dr. King, Johnson signed the Fair Housing Act – completly banning discrimination in the rent, sale, or financing of housing. More than a century after the Emancipation Proclamation, it was the last great battle in the war for legal equality, that so many others had given their lives for. One further Civil Rights Act was signed in 1991, but just a year later riots broke out across Los Angeles over the brutal police beating of a Black man, Rodney King. Although the US had finally been legally desegregated, it was widely seen as a sign that institutionalized racism was still very much alive, and kicking.

In 1958, Oklahoma school teacher Clara Luper and 13 students went to a lunch counter, sat down and refused to leave until they were served, paving the way to citywide desegregation

THE LAND OF THE FREE....?

The Thirteenth Amendment to the US Constitution may have abolished slavery, but its language created a loophole that has allowed the American penal system to repress minority classes ever since

Written by Will Lawrence

Convicts leased to harvest timber in Florida in 1915, providing a source of cheap labor to agricultural business in the South

114

Even the young were set to work in the fields after their arrest

According to the Bureau of Justice, one in three Black males can expect to spend time behind bars in the US

According to the US Bureau of Justice, one in every 17 White males is expected to spend time in prison during his lifetime. This is a shocking fact, given that America is the self-proclaimed land of the free, and yet it pales against facts cited by the same source which note that for Black males, the figure is one in three.

Black males comprise just 6.5 percent of the US population, and yet they constitute more than 40 percent of prison inmates. This is more than shocking; it is abhorrent, and lends considerable weight to the argument that the institution of American slavery remains active – albeit in a different form – despite the passing of the Thirteenth Amendment to the US Constitution more that 135 years ago.

The Thirteenth Amendment, which was passed by Congress on January 31, 1865, and came into law on December 18 of the same year, proclaims: "Neither slavery nor involuntary servitude, except as a punishment for crime whereof the party shall have been duly convicted, shall exist within the United States, or any place subject to their jurisdiction."

The criminality clause – "except as a punishment for crime whereof the party shall have been duly convicted" – is cited by commentators and civil rights advocates as a dangerous loophole, and they can point to powerful evidence which demonstrates that it has been exploited from the moment the amendment was passed.

The abolition of slavery crippled the Southern economy in the wake of the Civil War. Plantations, which were the bedrock of the economic system in the defeated states, lost their work force, prompting Southern lawmen and makers — many of whom were either plantation owners or were subject to intense lobbying, and their own prejudice — to immediately criminalize the emancipated Black population.

> ## "Black males comprise 6.5 percent of the US population, but 40 percent of prison inmates"

Black men were arrested in droves, accused of petty crimes like vagrancy and loitering, and once detained and interned were set to work once more, their newly found liberties evaporating far more quickly than they had arrived.

The perniciousness did not stop there. The mass arrests of the Black population fuelled the mythology of Black criminality, an idea that spread across America, reaching the states that had not employed an enslaved workforce and whose knowledge of the realities were slim.

This found full voice in D.W. Griffith's 1915 film *Birth of a Nation*, which demonized the Black male, casting him as a rapacious threat to White purity. The film was lauded for its technical accomplishment but its content was vile and polluted the minds of the White population in the Northern and Western states to which the Black population fled to escape the prejudice of the South.

The film was almost singularly responsible for the rebirth of the Ku Klux Klan; the iconography of the burning cross had never been part of Klan ritual and yet Griffith introduced it as a powerful cinematic image and it is still in use by sections of the white supremacy movement.

The period between Reconstruction and the outbreak of World War II saw countless lynchings and murders of Black males by White mobs, widely documented by newspaper photographs, along with the erosion of supposed liberties for

Images: Alamy

the Black populace via segregation and the Jim Crow laws. The murder of Emmett Till in August 1955 proved a watershed moment – images of his open-casket funeral were published – and boosted the strength of the Civil Rights Movement.

And yet, the myth of the Black criminal remained, and even politically neutral aspects of American history conspired against people of color. The Civil Rights Act, signed into law by President Lyndon Johnson on July 2, 1964, coincided with a dramatic upturn in crime; parallels with civil rights freedoms were incorrectly drawn.

In truth, the mid to late 1960s saw the baby boomer generation begin to enter adulthood and simple demographics were the determining factor behind burgeoning criminal activity. Simply put, more people equates to more crime.

In response to this rise in crime, President Nixon, who came to power in 1969, proclaimed the era of 'Law and Order' and what has come to be known as 'dog whistle politics', whereby coded and suggestive language was launched to garner support from the Southern states, without specifically naming the precise targets.

Nixon's cabinet attacked movements supporting Black power, women's rights, and the anti-war left. He denounced drugs as 'Public Enemy No.1', and introduced mass incarceration for relatively low-level drug offenses.

The liberal left was attacked for marijuana possession, the Black population for heroin, and in the ten years from 1970 to 1980 the prison population, which had remained relatively static during the course of the 20th century, surged from 357,000 to 513,000. The die had been cast.

Nixon launched the rhetorical war on drugs but it was President Reagan, who held office from 1981 to 1989, who executed the literal war. It was during the 1980s that crack cocaine came to the fore as America's bête noire. It was cheaper, more addictive, and far less socially acceptable than powdered cocaine and prompted the introduction of mandatory sentencing, which cut swathes through poorer White, Black, and Latin communities.

The war on crack was an attack on a specific class. The sentence for one ounce of crack possession was the same as the sentence for 100 ounces of cocaine. Richer White people, who were more likely than their poorer Black counterparts to abuse the latter, were not targeted or prosecuted to the same degree. By 1985, the prison population had bubbled to almost 760,000.

Ten years later it stood at almost 1.2 million as even the more liberal arm of the American political system became swept up in the need to present itself as tough on crime. It was a Democrat, President Bill Clinton (1993-2001), who introduced the 1994 Crime Bill, which included the federally backed 'three-strikes' provision,

Work gangs comprised of minorities, like this one at Limestone County Correctional Facility near Huntsville, Alabama, are still part of the American corrections system

mandating life sentences for criminals convicted of a violent felony after two or more prior convictions, including drug crimes.

The Bill saw a colossal expansion of the prison system and militarized the police force, with even small, semi-rural precincts armed with SWAT provisions. It positively incentivized incarceration and trawled the most vulnerable American citizenry; it was overwhelmingly biased against people of color. By 2000, the prison population stood at more than 2 million.

Four years later, the figure boomed to more than 2.3 million, rapidly fuelling what is known as America's prison-industrial complex (PIC). This was not a new concept but awareness of the PIC has grown with commentators attributing the rapid expansion of the US inmate population to the political influence of private prison companies and businesses that supply goods and services to government prison agencies for profit.

Privately owned companies that form the PIC build and run prisons and must ensure that their investment is protected. They require full prisons. It should, therefore, come as no surprise that these companies seek to influence policy and they have been given this opportunity via the American Legislative Exchange Council (ALEC), which is comprised of politicians and major corporations. ALEC provides US big business with an opportunity to introduce legislative ideas, which are then voted upon – with politicians and business leaders voting on equal terms. If an idea succeeds in the voting phase, US politicians bid to bring the laws to Congress.

Companies like Walmart and Coca-Cola have been members of ALEC, along with many others, including what was known as the Corrections Corporation of America (CCA). CCA, now rebranded as CoreCivic, was a long-time member of ALEC and currently describes itself as "the nation's leading provider of high-quality corrections and detention management." In 2010, excellent journalism from NPR highlighted how CCA, using its influence via ALEC, benefitted

Barack Obama became the first sitting US president to visit a correctional facility during his bid to highlight the need for prison reform in 2015

D.W. Griffith's *Birth of a Nation* almost single-handedly relaunched the KKK in early 20th century America

THE BIRTH OF A NATION

"THE SUPREME PICTURE OF ALL TIME"

NEW YORK MAIL
MAY 4TH 1921

hugely from Arizona Senate Bill 1070, the strictest anti-illegal immigration measure ever passed in the US. The detention of illegal immigrants in Arizona, who were held at CCA facilities, was worth an astonishing $11 million per month to the company.

CCA left ALEC in the aftermath of the NPR exposé but other members of the PIC remain, such as the American Bail Corporation (ABC), and critics note how a softening of laws governing parole are designed to benefit ABC more than those released from prisons.

And many companies, whether ALEC members or not, reap vast benefits from free prison labor, with the likes of Boeing, Microsoft, JC Penney, Victoria's Secret, and the US military all having used inmates to manufacture their products, paying them pennies on the dollar. There is profit to be made from punishment.

It is free prison labor that draws the most overt comparison to slave labor but there is more to slavery than servitude. Slavery dehumanizes and represses, depriving victims of rights readily enjoyed by those who are free, and one only need consider the 'scarlet letter' that is stitched into the lives of convicted felons even upon release.

Depending on the state that convicts, felons might lose their right to vote either temporarily or permanently, while the majority of those convicted of crimes report the difficulties they face when seeking employment after release.

Aspects of Jim Crow are still alive in the US, and the land of the free has not abolished its racial caste; it has simply redesigned it. The Thirteenth Amendment granted freedom to the enslaved but has also attacked those liberties across a complicated and often cruel history that is still evolving to this day.

The role of the media

The inspiration for – and the evidence cited in – our main feature article comes from *13th*, the 2016 American documentary film by director Ava DuVernay, which examines the intersection of race, justice, and mass incarceration in the US. It earned an Oscar nomination for Best Documentary and won the Primetime Emmy for Outstanding Documentary, highlighting its position as another important cornerstone in the media-history of American slavery.

Filmmaking is among one of the modern media's most influential tools – there is currently a host of excellent non-fiction movies documenting the injustices served to minority communities in the US.

In the early years of mass media, though the recorded history of slavery could not compete with the propaganda of *Birth of a Nation*, it was still employed to highlight the blight. In the 19th century, autobiographies and slave narratives emerged, such as those written by Frederick Douglass, as well as published images, like the photographs depicting the latticed scarring on the back of Slave Gordon.

As the century turned, the printed mass media and then the television camera forced America to face the horrors still being perpetrated against Black communities. The film images and published images from Emmett Till's 1955 funeral proved a major catalyst in the birth of the Civil Rights Movement as shocking TV images of police brutality forced the country to confront inequality.

In the modern era, the camera phone has shone yet another light on the issue; the footage capturing police officers killing Oscar Grant and Eric Garner are just two of the examples shown in *13th*. The list of examples is long and painful to watch and it's shocking to note that the death of George Floyd in 2020 mirrors that of Garner's in 2014. It is the role of media, in all its forms, to keep the spotlight focused.

FROM SLAVE TO CRIMINAL WITH ONE AMENDMENT

13TH | OCTOBER 7

Ava DuVernay's documentary provides powerful evidence of the continuation of slavery and repression in the US via the penal system

A demonstrator with letters 'BLM' written on her forehead attends a protest at the Place de la République square, in Paris, June 2020

LEGACY & LASTING IMPACT

An exploration into the lasting legacies of more than 400 years of transatlantic trafficking of enslaved African people

Written by Josephine Hall

We can't be sure how many African people were enslaved during more than 400 years of the transatlantic trafficking and enslavement they endured. Most records only count the people that arrived alive, not the millions who died during raiding and transporting while still in Africa, or during the horrifying journey across the Atlantic known as the Middle Passage. Estimates vary from 12 million to 100 million people. UNESCO estimates that 30 million African people were forcibly uprooted from their homeland during this time. Given the level of trauma, death, and oppression over such an extended period of time, there has been a deep, lasting impact experienced in the ancestral communities of both the captives and captors, around the world. From the west coast of Africa (where most enslaved people were taken from), to countries like Britain, Brazil, France, and the United States (who were some of the main perpetrators of the atrocities of the transatlantic slave trade, and also where many of the African diaspora now reside), to the countries in the Caribbean and South America that were once colonies of Britain or other European countries, the lasting legacies of hundreds of years of trafficking and enslaving African people are woven intricately into the fabric of our societies.

Image: Alamy

SYSTEMIC RACISM

The terms 'systemic racism' or 'institutional racism' are now widely understood and there has been a lot of research that evidences their existence within structures and systems across the world. It is increasingly accepted that there is a direct connection between these structural inequalities and the institutional racism experienced by the African diaspora today.

The Covid-19 crisis exposed some of these more hidden inequalities – a 2020 study estimated that Black people in the US were 3.57 times more likely to die from Covid-19 than White people, UK Government statistics showed Covid was also more lethal for BAME people in the UK, and a Brazilian study found that 55 percent of Black and mixed-race Covid patients died, compared to 38 percent of White patients.

The disparity in these figures between ethnic groups is no surprise when we look at the other documented figures around healthcare inequalities between different groups. For example, there have been several research studies in the US that have shown that Black adults and children are less likely to be given pain medication. A 2016 study discovered that many White medical students held the same false beliefs (such as Black people having thicker skin or less sensitive nerve endings) that were used by some 19th-century doctors to justify the inhumane treatment of enslaved people.

In 2021, the British government published a controversial report that claimed institutional racism did not exist. It received extensive criticism, with anti-racism campaigners describing it as a 'whitewash' of the lived experiences of people of color and UN experts calling it an "attempt to normalize white supremacy."

A 2021 survey of nearly 1,300 workers from BME backgrounds in Britain, carried out by the Trades Union Congress (TUC), found that more than a third reported that they had been unfairly turned down for a job, a quarter said they had been singled out for redundancy and 15 percent of

> ## "Black people in the US were 3.57 times more likely to die from Covid-19"

A 'Code Noir' document from 1743. Code Noir was passed by the French King Louis XIV in 1685 defining the rules of slavery in the French colonial empire

Branding enslaved people after they have been bought for plantation work – from *The History of Slavery and the Slave Trade* by W.O. Blake, 1859

The 'Plantation Police' inspect the passes of enslaved Black men in 19th century Louisiana

African Americans are around three times more likely to be killed by the police than White Americans

those who said they'd been harassed left their job because of racist treatment.

Many other indicators of how enslaving Africans until the 19th century still influences the structural racism found in today's institutions can be found across housing, education, employment, and many other areas of society – in Britain, Europe, the United States, and around the world.

WHAT DO THE POLICE HAVE TO DO WITH IT?

In 1661, the British colony of Barbados passed its first 'slave law' – a special set of rules for "the good regulating and ordering" of enslaved people. Equivalent measures, sometimes called 'slave codes', were adopted in English and European colonies around the world. In 1797, Patrick Colquhoun – a London magistrate who had previously served as an agent for British cotton manufacturers and owned shares in sugar plantations in Jamaica – published *A Treatise on the Police of the Metropolis*, which later inspired Robert Peel to initiate the establishment of the London MetropolitanPolice in 1829.

In the US in 1829, a Black abolitionist in Boston named David Walker published a call for rebellion. Within the year, he was found dead and a series of mob attacks against other abolitionists in Boston followed. Walker's words had terrified Southern enslavers, and in response the governor of North Carolina formed a statewide 'patrol committee'. Even as the main players in the transatlantic slave trade began to abolish slavery throughout the 1800s, it did little to change the core purpose of policing – especially in the US, where all expressions of Black freedom were criminalized. Domestic security forces, which began as White vigilante groups, soon became formal law enforcement agencies and were designed not to ensure law and order for all citizens, but to 'protect' White communities from Black people.

DO THE POLICE OPERATE DIFFERENTLY NOW?

Centuries after the first police forces were created to control enslaved people and the working class, we can still see evidence of unequal and racist policing all over the world.

Images: Alamy (Code Noir branding); Getty Images (Plantation Police, child)

Reparations Now!

A speaker at The Afrikan Emancipation Day Reparations March in Brixton, 2019 – calling on the government for "holistic reparatory justice" for the legacy of slavery

Black people have been calling for financial reparations throughout history, along with their calls for freedom and equality. Yet, this has repeatedly been met with resistance from governments around the world.

Writing for *The Guardian* in 2020, journalist and broadcaster Afua Hirsch wrote, "The debate about reparations has, conveniently, been branded extreme and unrealistic by those who don't want to pay them. We happily listen to the heir to the throne – who on Windrush Day said Britain owed a "debt of gratitude" to the people of the Caribbean – while ignoring the reality that what Britain owes is, in fact, a straight-up financial debt."

Despite the resistance of Western nations to the topic they have been comfortable with receiving compensation themselves. France extorted huge sums from Haiti for over a century, as reparations for loss of earnings when enslaved Africans on the island overthrew their enslavers. In the United States, the Confederates who lost the civil war received compensation for their loss of 'property' (i.e. enslaved people). Similar examples can be found in the records of other countries, including the Netherlands, Colombia, Peru and Brazil.

Writing for the *New Statesman* in 2014, Priyamvada Gopal commented on the transatlantic trade of enslaved Africans' crucial role in helping to set up capitalism itself – the system that we all live under today. She wrote, "Maybe this is why there is such resistance at governmental and corporate levels to opening up the question of reparations. It might lead us to ask why large corporations, like slave owners, receive bailouts or compensation for losses incurred, as did slave owners, but people who inherit landlessness and poverty, whether descendants of slaves or not, are repeatedly told not to expect help or benefits, to look to themselves."

away because there's a Black person in power, because, in fact, the societies were built on this."

In 2021, the United Nations Human Rights Council adopted a milestone UN resolution to investigate the root causes of systemic racism and police violence. Led by three independent experts, and brought forward by the Group of African States, the investigation aims to examine systemic racism, particularly in law enforcement. It will also look into government responses to peaceful anti-racism protests, discriminatory policing, and other human rights violations against African people and their descendants, all around the globe.

DEFUND THE POLICE?

In light of the violence perpetrated by police officers, and the continued lack of protection for racialized communities, there have been calls to defund, or even entirely abolish, the police, from human rights and racial justice campaigners around the world. To some, this sounds radical. But advocates explain that it is about instead investing in services specifically designed to address issues in the community, such as rehabilitation, homelessness, and mental health crisis. The concept of complete abolition may seem drastic, but the goal of the movement is simply to get to a place where police aren't needed, due to the strategic redistribution of resources, funding, and power into specialized community-based alternatives.

In 2020, *The Guardian* reported that in the three months following George Floyd's murder, a dozen local governments in the US moved to reduce their police budgets by more than $1.4

In the US, African Americans are 20 percent more likely to have their vehicles pulled over and about three times more likely than White Americans to be killed by police. In the UK in 2018-2019, Black people were eight times more likely to be stopped and searched by police than White people, and 43 times more likely to be stopped under the use of Section 60 – which allows police to stop people without suspicion that a crime is actually taking place. Metropolitan Police officers are also four times more likely to use force against Black people, compared to White people, according to Greater London Authority estimates released in 2020. Brazil is the country with the highest number of killings perpetrated by the police worldwide. In Rio de Janeiro, more than three quarters of the

close to 9,000 people killed by police between 2010 and 2020 were Black men.

Even in many Black majority countries, there is a historical disregard for Black life left over from colonial times that continues to form the basis of policing. Victims of police brutality in Jamaica are usually poor, and because of the distinct connection between class and color on the island, usually dark-skinned. The colorism that plagues Jamaican society has its origins in the history of mixed-race children fathered by White enslavers – often as a result of sexual violence – that were given special privileges, such as exemption from working in the fields. When talking to *The World* in 2020, author and University of Pennsylvania professor, Deborah Thomas said, "It [anti-Black violence] doesn't go

People holding a 'Defund The Police' sign at a protest in Brooklyn in June 2020

billion – seeming to mark a significant shift in US politics. There have also been calls to defund the police in Britain, with organizations such as the youth advocacy group The 4Front Project campaigning for funding to be shifted from police forces into projects aimed at improving healthcare, education, and social services. Temi Mwale, executive director of The4FP told CBS News in 2020, "We do not want to invest in institutions that are inherently violent, inherently racist, and that continue to perpetuate cycles of harm, violence and abuse in our communities. We would rather invest in services that. . . increase our protection and safety, that increase our ability to move forward and fight for racial justice."

In both the US and Britain, budget cuts to psychiatric services have resulted in police taking on more of a role when managing those in psychological distress. In 2015, a *Washington Post* analysis found that 25 percent of those shot and killed by police in the United States, within a six-month period, were experiencing a mental health crisis. Other countries, such as Sweden, operate differently – since 2015, they have deployed mental health professionals onto the streets, without

police officers – freeing up police resources to focus on the fields they have expertice in.

BLACK LIVES MATTER

In 2013 in the US, Alicia Garza, Patrisse Cullors, and Opal Tometi created #BlackLivesMatter, in response to the acquittal of George Zimmerman for the murder of Trayvon Martin. In 2014, following the fatal shooting of Mike Brown by Ferguson police officer Darren Wilson, BLM gained national attention after street demonstrations were organized to support the Ferguson community. Since then, BLM has developed and organized into a decentralized political and social movement fighting against legacies of slavery – police brutality and racism against Black people.

Since George Floyd's murder by Minneapolis police officer Derek Chauvin in 2020, the movement has gained further international attention and an estimated 15 to 26 million people participated in the 2020 Black Lives Matter protests in the United States – making it one of the largest movements in the country's history. BLM comprises many views and

Jamaican activist Marcus Garvey argued that people of African descent should return to the continent

Dancers during Brazil's President Luiz Inacio Lula da Silva's meeting with the Tabom people in Accra, 2008

"Black Lives Matter has developed into a decentralized movement fighting against legacies of slavery"

demands, but the focus is on criminal justice reform. There are also active and growing BLM movements happening all around the world, including in Britain, Brazil, Colombia, Denmark, France, and Canada.

MONEY, MONEY, MONEY

In the United States, the origins of the staggering Black-White wealth gap can be traced back to the country's inception. African Americans' efforts to build wealth have been obstructed in many ways. From mismanagement of banks, to violent massacres such as in Tulsa's Greenwood District in 1921 (often referred to as 'Black Wall Street'), to countless discriminatory policies, such as Jim Crow's 'Black Codes' and 'redlining' – wealth has been systematically taken from Black communities in the US for centuries.

In 2016, taxpayers in the UK found out that they'd only recently finished paying off the 'compensation' awarded to slave owners after the abolition of slavery in 1833. In a now deleted tweet, the British Government's Treasury Department tried to offer a positive spin for its followers: "Here's today's surprising #FridayFact. Millions of you helped end the slave trade through your taxes." The tweet went on to explain how in 1833, Britain borrowed £20 million (40 percent of the national budget, and around £17 billion in modern terms) in order to compensate 46,000 enslavers for their loss of property. The loan was one of the largest in history, and was not paid off until 2015, meaning that living British citizens – including the descendants of those that were enslaved – have been helping to pay for the lives of traffickers and enslavers, and their descendants, for centuries. Despite the misleading name of the 'Slave Compensation Act', the former enslaved people were not compensated.

Since the 2020 Black Lives Matter protests swept the world after George Floyd's murder in the US, several financial institutions in the UK issued public apologies for their ties to the trading of enslaved people. Some have also announced they will stop displaying images of former governors connected to enslavement in their buildings. But many say this is not enough. A 2020 Runnymede report "The Color of Money: How racial inequalities obstruct a fair and resilient economy" found that the stark disparities between the financial outcomes of different ethnic groups has emerged from historical racial inequalities and colonial history. It found that African and Bangladeshi households hold ten times less wealth than White people, as well as persistent inequalities across education, health, employment, poverty, and housing. University College London's 2012 'Legacies of British Slave Ownership' project showed that 10 to 20 percent of Britain's wealthy have significant links to slavery.

"In 2016, UK taxpayers found out they'd only recently finished paying off the 'compensation' awarded to slave owners after the abolition of slavery"

Black Lives Matter supporters take to the streets in Los Angeles during the first anniversary of George Floyd's death, May 25, 2021

The removal of a statue of Confederate General Robert E. Lee begins in Richmond, Virginia, in September 2021

ARE APOLOGIES ENOUGH?

Many anti-racism campaigners feel that governments and powerful organizations are not doing enough to take responsibility for their links to the transatlantic trading of enslaved people.

Speaking to Reuters in 2020, Professor Sir Hilary Beckles – a Barbadian historian and vice-chancellor of the University of the West Indies – said that many British and European firms "drank from the well of Caribbean slavery" and "all the institutions that created this mess really have to come and help in practical ways to clean it up." He called on British and European firms to fund development projects in the Caribbean, saying: "It is not enough to make your apology as a public spectacle, it is not enough to present it as a public relations exercise."

In 2006, the Church of England publicly apologized to the descendants of enslaved people, after acknowledging that its missionary group had inherited three sugar estates in the Caribbean which were run for the Church with the forced labor of enslaved people, branded with the word 'society' on their chests. In 2020, *The Telegraph* reported that nearly 100 clergymen also benefitted individually from the trafficking and trading of enslaved people. A spokesperson from the Church said it was "a source of shame" that some within the Church had "actively perpetrated slavery and profited from it."

During 2020 protests against police brutality and structural racism, protestors took matters

> ## "Over 170 Confederate monuments were removed between June 2020 and June 2021"

into their own hands – by taking down or defacing monuments celebrating colonial figures, all over the world. Governments soon started to remove statues themselves. In the US, over 170 Confederate monuments were removed between June 2020 and June 2021, according to data from the Southern Poverty Law Center.

In 2020, wires and guards were deployed in São Paulo to protect a statue of Borba Gato – one of Brazil's most prominent enslavers. In 2021, the monument was set on fire by campaigners – but the event was quickly controlled and the statue remained in place.

In 2021, Germany announced it would return hundreds of stolen artifacts to Benin, in West Africa, that had been pillaged, distributed, and sold amongst the various White European nations during the late 19th century. The

Protesters throw statue of prominent enslaver Edward Colston into Bristol harbor, during a Black Lives Matter protest in 2020

BELOW A plaque in abolitionist David Walker's honor at the site of his former home on Joy Street in Boston

8 BELKNAP STREET
DAVID WALKER c1796 - 1830

In 1829 published "Appeal to the Colored Citizens of the World" decrying American slavery, racial hatred, and summoning his fellow African Americans to resist. Possession of the Appeal was a crime in the South. A bounty was placed on him by Georgia slave owners.

The Heritage Guild, Inc

University of Aberdeen also announced it would return a Benin Bronze to Nigeria, more than a century after Britain looted and auctioned it.

THE LASTING IMPACT IN AFRICA

The transatlantic trafficking of enslaved Africans left an extensive impact in the countries that people were taken from – mainly on the west coast of the continent. This ubiquitous influence spreads across economic, institutional, political, and cultural spheres.

For example, we can look at some of the long-term impacts of the sudden influx of firearms into African countries – a direct consequence of the trading of enslaved people with Europe and Britain. It is estimated that 20 million guns were imported to Africa in the second half of the 18th century, many of which were manufactured in Birmingham, UK. In a 2012 paper, "The Gun-Slave Cycle in the 18th Century British Slave Trade in Africa", Warren Whatley found evidence of a 'gun-slave cycle' – African people being captured by other Africans and traded in exchange for firearms, which sustained internal wars. This mass importation of guns in exchange for people altered the conduct of warfare across Africa, and changed the balance of power between regions. With their new weapons, warfare became increasingly attractive to kings and rulers. Wars created captives – and therefore, potential enslaved people to traffic and profit from. The demands of the

trafficking business destabilized existing kingdoms, and existing systems of governance and social bonds based on kinship, consent, and trust were destroyed.

The increase in wars intensified economic inequalities already present among leaders and kingdoms, as well as creating additional problems. Nathan Nunn presented a systematic empirical analysis of the effects of this on current economic performance ("The Long-Term Effects of Africa's Slave Trades", 2008). It showed a robust negative relationship between the number of enslaved people exported from a country and per capita income in 2000, despite evidence that the trafficking was more intense in the most developed and most densely populated areas in Africa.

ONGOING TRAUMA

The most significant and devastating impacts of the transatlantic trafficking empires were felt by the millions of individuals that were enslaved. It has also left a lasting legacy of trauma within the African diaspora, still felt today and exacerbated by ongoing social, political, and economic inequalities. The term 'post-traumatic slave syndrome' was coined by Dr. Joy DeGruy in 2005 and described as "a condition that exists when a population has experienced multigenerational trauma. . . and continues to experience oppression and institutionalised racism today." For many, the wounds of slavery are still open and festering.

MODERN SLAVERY

Systems of enslavement and what is referred to as 'modern slavery' are still present in many African societies, as well as in other countries around the world. In 2018, the Global Slavery Index (GSI) published these staggering statistics: "An estimated 40.3 million men, women, and children were victims of modern slavery on any given day in 2016. Of these, 24.9 million people were in forced labor and 15.4 million people were living in a forced marriage. Women and girls are vastly over-represented, making up 71 percent of victims. Modern slavery is most prevalent in Africa, followed by Asia and the Pacific region."

Despite the practices of enslavement still being widespread globally, it remains a largely invisible issue. Partly because the people it disproportionately affects are the most marginalized members of society – ethnic minorities, women, and children.

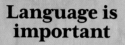

Language is important

Many academics and anti-racism campaigners have called for an increased awareness around how we speak about the 400-plus years of transatlantic trafficking of enslaved Africans. It is a part of the larger debate over 'people first' language – e.g. 'a person with diabetes' rather than 'a diabetic person' – which seeks to center the humanity of the individuals, rather than characteristics. Although calls for changes in language are often met with resistance, history has shown that we are capable of proactively making these changes and it is now second nature to use terms that were once controversial, such as 'African American' or 'firefighter'.

Founded in 1909, the NAACP is the USA's oldest and largest civil rights organization. On their website, is a community-sourced guide called "Writing About Slavery/Teaching About Slavery: This Might Help" (P. Gabrielle Foreman, et al). Here are some suggested takeaways:

- To avoid the objectification of African people, say '*enslaved people*' or '*captives*' rather than '*slaves*'
- Likewise, we can say '*trafficking of enslaved Africans*' rather than '*slave trade*'
- We can use '*enslaver*' or '*those who claimed people as property/held people in slavery*' instead of '*master*' or '*owner*'
- Instead of '*runaway slave*' or '*rebel*', we can say '*self-liberated*'/ '*self-emancipated*' or '*freedom fighter*'
- Avoid saying '*slave mistress*' or '*enslaved mistress*' and instead name the sexual violence/conditions
- Consider using not only '*stolen labor*' but also '*stolen labor, knowledge and skills*'

NAACP President Cornell William Brooks speaking during a press conference on June 19, 2015 in Charleston, South Carolina

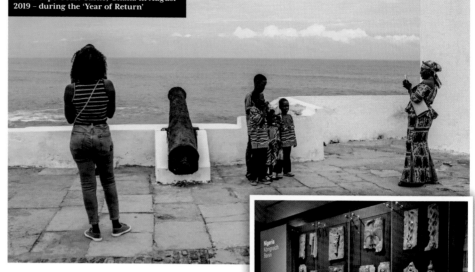

African-American visitors pose for pictures at the Cape Coast Castle, Ghana in August 2019 – during the 'Year of Return'

Bronze sculptures looted by British soldiers from the Kingdom of Benin in 1897 hang on display in the 'Where Is Africa' exhibition at the Linden Museum in Stuttgart, Germany – before being returned to Nigeria in 2022

BACK TO AFRICA

Amongst some of the earliest returnees to Africa were a group of Afro-Brazilians, who later became known as Tabom people, in 1835. After the Malê revolt, thousands of free and enslaved Africans emigrated from Brazil to present-day Nigeria, Benin, Ghana, and Togo.

Throughout the 19th century, the United States was responsible for several programs that encouraged the return of Black people in the US to African countries. Led by organizations like the American Colonization Society, this impulse resulted in the founding of West African colonies such as Sierra Leone in 1787 and Liberia in 1819.

Then in the 20th century, Jamaican activist Marcus Garvey and his organization the Universal Negro Improvement Association (UNIA) led one of the largest mass movements in African-American history. Although a divisive figure, criticized by many in the Black community due to his collaboration with white supremacists, UNIA attracted followers throughout the Caribbean, Africa, South America, and Great Britain. Garvey's 'Back to Africa' message appealed to Black people around the world who needed an alternative to the oppressive societies they lived in, and would go on to influence the framework of Rastafarianism.

The Rastafari movement developed in Jamaica in the 1930s, and although it doesn't promote all the same views that Garvey did and in fact Garvey is said to have been a critic of the religion, some Rastas today still consider him a prophet. Leonard E. Barrett Sr. wrote in *The Rastafarians* (1997), "The movement views Ethiopia as the promised land, the place where Black people will be repatriated through a wholesale exodus from all Western countries where they have been in exile (slavery)." In 1948, Emperor Haile Selassie of Ethiopia donated some land in Shashamane to Rastafarians for all African-Caribbean people to return to. After his 1966 tour of the Caribbean, thousands relocated to Shashamane. The emphasis on the need for physical repatriation to Africa has declined in recent years, with many now following the call to 'return to Africa' in a more spiritual sense.

In 2019, Ghana hosted the 'Year of Return' – a 365-day program of activities to commemorate the 400th anniversary of the first recorded enslaved Africans arriving in British North America. It welcomed people of African descent from around the world to return 'home'. In 2020, Ghana announced a ten-year 'Beyond the Return' project which aims to provide a platform for engagement among the African diaspora worldwide.

LASTING LEGACY

There are many more legacies of the transatlantic trafficking of enslaved Africans that haven't been explored in this feature, as the lasting impacts are so huge, widespread, and complex. We all have a responsibility to educate ourselves on those legacies and to consider what actions we can take to help create a more equal society that isn't modelled on such a horrifying history.

Images: Getty Images (David Walker, Ghana, bronze sculptures), Alamy (Colston statue, Cornell William Brooks)